"*The Sword of Moses* is one of the most intrigu[ing] from late antiquity. In this work, Harold Roth material through its sources, development, and accessible to the modern reader. In a lucid and scholarly style, the author opens the door to practice of the magic of the Sword today. This is an excellent book and a welcome addition to the literature on Jewish magic and grimoires, which I wholeheartedly recommend."

—David Rankine, author of *The Grimoire Encyclopedia*

"In *The Magic of the Sword of Moses*, Harold Roth presents a well-organized, insightful, and informative guide to an important first-century Jewish manual of magic, a critical edition of which was recently produced by Joseph Peterson, who contributed the foreword here. This is an excellent addition to any modern grimoirist's bookshelf, outlining as it does the history, background and, above all, use of *The Sword of Moses*. This significant work enables us to understand the use of the Sword in the past, while encouraging and assisting active engagement with it by practitioners today."

—Jake Stratton-Kent, author of The Encyclopedia Goetica series

"What a fascinating book, a treasure trove of both history and spells. More than any purely scholarly or purely magical text, *The Magic of the Sword of Moses* brings ancient Jewish magic to life in all its uniqueness and power."

—Rachel Pollack, author of *Seventy-Eight Degrees of Wisdom* and *A Walk Through the Forest of Souls*

"I have probably learned more about Jewish magic from *The Magic of the Sword of Moses* than from any other single book I have read in the past. Apart from the translation of the text itself and the modern applications that Harold suggests, the context that is given is extensive and delicious. I particularly appreciate the passages detailing the thoughts of different rabbis on magic and the relationship between angels and humans. Ancient works of magic are sometimes difficult to use in the modern day without significant changes, but The Sword of Moses can be wielded by anyone willing to follow the instructions and put in the effort. The spells in this text are as relevant today as they were fifteen hundred years ago when they were written."

—Jason Miller, author of *Consorting with Spirits*

"Harold Roth provides a coherent, digestible, and wonderfully entertaining guide to *The Sword of Moses*. This is the perfect tome for any Jewish magical practitioner or occultist, and it is a treat to live in this exciting time when authors like Roth are making new sense out of such seminal grimoires and ancient magical texts. There are several things from this book that I have already adopted into my own study and practice."

—Cooper Kaminsky, professional diviner and teacher of Jewish folk magic

"*The Magic of the Sword of Moses* is the rare book on Jewish magick that derives from both a scholarly and a practitioner perspective. Harold Roth unpacks scholarly aspects of Jewish magick and where this text fits into that lineage, but also provides context and his unique insights as a practitioner. This book will be a treasure to anyone interested in the study or practice of Jewish magick."

—Kohenet Ketzirah Lesser, founder of *Devotaj Sacred Arts*

"Harold Roth's interpretation of the medieval Jewish grimoire, *The Sword of Moses* is a must read for anyone interested in Jewish magic or the broader grimoire tradition. Providing a great deal of useful cultural and historical context, it walks the reader through the straightforward preparatory rituals, and then provides a dazzling assortment of spells which can be used as is or as inspiration for the development of personal methods. Of course, there are some places where Mr. Roth and I disagree (as we say "two Jews, three opinions") but he is never dogmatic. Instead, like the original author of *The Sword*, he provides all the necessary information to help readers make their own decisions about what practices are right for them. I cannot recommend the book highly enough!"

—Sara Mastros, author of *The Big Book of Magical Incense*

"Harold Roth expertly shares a system of magic unfamiliar to most of us who have worked with the usual grimoires. He explains both the historic and magickal context as well as how to put it into practical use, a feature missing from most modern editions of classic texts. A true magical scholar, Roth both educates and inspires, sharing from his experience."

—Christopher Penczak, author of the *Temple of Witchcraft* series

THE MAGIC OF
The SWORD
of MOSES

THE MAGIC OF
The SWORD
of MOSES

A Practical Guide to
Its Spells, Amulets, and Ritual

HAROLD ROTH

FOREWORD BY JOSEPH PETERSON

WEISER BOOKS

This edition first published in 2022 by Weiser Books, an imprint of
Red Wheel/Weiser, LLC
With offices at:
65 Parker Street, Suite 7
Newburyport, MA 01950
www.redwheelweiser.com

ISBN: 978-1-57863-726-3
Library of Congress Cataloging-in-Publication Data available upon request.

Cover design by Kathryn Sky-Peck
Cover and interior calligraphy by Harold Roth
Interior by Debby Dutton
Typeset in Adobe Garamond and Orpheus

Printed in the United States of America
IBI
10 9   8 7 6 5 4 3 2 1

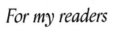

For my readers

CONTENTS

FOREWORD

The Sword of Moses is one of the earliest surviving handbooks of Jewish magic and perhaps the most significant. This well-researched book by Harold Roth should be of interest to a wide audience. Although focused primarily on *The Sword*, his approach and insights go beyond this specific text.

Most surviving Western magic texts exhibit significant Jewish influences and incorporate many Jewish elements, such as the use of Psalms and especially Hebrew names and descriptive titles of God. Unfortunately, those late grimoires often suffer from long lines of errors by copyists who lacked Hebrew skills. So what was once readily understood by the original audience is now beyond recognition. Those readers also came with a background quite different from modern ones. What the original author could safely assume about his readers no longer applies to modern audiences. This poses a big challenge to editors and translators: In addition to a coherent translation, they must provide context that the reader can relate to. Often there are still gaps, especially for would-be practitioners and those interested in historical reenactment. Some gaps of course can no longer be bridged, key elements having been lost through textual corruption or lack of knowledge of the original assumptions. This basically forces readers and would-be practitioners to make leaps and adaptations.

In this book, Harold Roth uses a number of approaches to bridge these gaps and make *The Sword of Moses* more approachable.

The text of *The Sword of Moses* is intelligently assembled. Its compiler demonstrates knowledge of a variety of older sources, such as earlier amulets and material in multiple languages—Hebrew, Aramaic, and Greek. Its origin is perhaps as early as the late first millennium. Its popularity in ancient times is attested by the fact that excerpts were found in eleventh- and twelfth-century manuscripts in the early Jewish collection known as the Cairo Genizah.

There is much of interest for us here as well.

To the historian, it offers a catalog of what services a historical practitioner offered to his community and what kinds of services were in demand. The community served seems to have concerned itself more with gaining knowledge, wisdom, and improving memory than becoming wealthy. It is interesting to speculate why there are no spells for wealth, treasure-finding, or gambling to be found here; might these be more dangerous offerings for the professional magician? However, some of the spells that *are* found in the text have distinctly harmful intent; might their inclusion be intended to impress prospective clients and not for actual use—aimed to create an air of danger? Or might the intent have been to impress would-be practitioners regarding the theoretical power of this kind of magic?

To the practitioner, the methods found in *The Sword* have a lot of appeal. The preparation process is relatively effortless, involving only three days of prayers and ablutions. Contrast this with the nine-day preparation in the *Key of Solomon*, the seventy-two-day preparation in *The Sworn Book of Honorius*, and the six- to eighteen-month preparation in the method of Abramelin. No confederates need to be conscripted. Moreover, the spells don't employ any exotic ingredients or expensive ritual implements. Instead, they rely primarily on consecrations, prayers, and sacred names. The theory is coherent, the

THE MAGIC OF THE SWORD OF MOSES

methods fascinating and appealing. For example, to reverse a spell, one writes or recites the names in reverse order. I was especially fascinated by the ritual gesture to trigger some spells, namely bending the little finger of your left hand.

This book should also interest those concerned with creating fantasy fiction and film who want to add depth and realism to their works or fans who want to complement their understanding of the history and practice of magic.

Harold Roth brings a wealth of knowledge and experience to help readers better understand and use the text. He examines what would really be needed to reenact the described rituals as closely as possible. This often sheds unexpected light on the text. His familiarity with many of the ingredients and their properties, such as the many species of artemisia, qualifies his recommendations. Likewise, his discussion of the properties of various ink ingredients is useful. Many other practical tips are included. For example, daytime fasting, which is required for preparation for the rituals, could be shortened by operating in the winter. He sensibly advises complementing supernatural methods with conventional health care, including mental health care.

Roth goes on to show how spells can be adapted to a modern context and provides rationales for such adaptations. Many of his insights are relevant to any modern magicians, not just Sword workers. Roth's approach to adapting ancient spells could be applied to other magic texts as well.

Many magic texts can be daunting, perhaps intentionally to mystify practitioners or discourage them from trying the spells themselves.

The text of *The Sword* has an intentional arrangement well suited to encourage people to browse the catalog of spells but then to rely on the expert.

Harold Roth has gone beyond the ancient text of *The Sword of Moses* and its assumptions and provided suggestions for how it can be adapted to modern situations. The result makes this interesting text come alive and practical for a wide audience.

Joseph Peterson, author of the *Elucidation of Necromancy*

INTRODUCTION

The first time I came across *The Sword of Moses,* it was in the form of Moses Gaster's translation published in 1896 as a small book.[1] It was a gloomy day, and I went with some friends to a university library to poke around. They were in the history section, but I went for the occult books. I saw the word *Moses* on a binding and pulled the slim book off the shelf. It was old, with bumped corners and a musty smell, but those characteristics made it seem all the more valuable. I thought surely it must contain vital magical practices that would give power to my own magic.

I took it to an isolated carrel and paged through it, excited. For once I had my hands on a grimoire that was not Christian, as was the case with the medieval and later grimoires I'd come across.

But it was like catching sight of an enticing landscape surrounded by barbed wire, deep ditches, and rusty railroad tracks. The magic was just over there, but there was no way to get to it from where I was. For one thing, all the Hebrew was transliterated into Roman letters without any vowels. With my prayer-book Hebrew, I couldn't even begin to know what the words were or how to say them.

*Worse, I saw that the translator had replaced many of the divine names, which I knew even then must be the actual motor of the magic of the work, with X's. At the time, I thought the X's were there

---

* It was only many years later that I learned that these words were not meant to be all that intelligible, as they were primarily the language of angels, whose speech we cannot know.

because the original was illegible in those parts. I didn't realize then that the translator had deliberately morphed the divine names into X's for reasons of his own.

Here was, in some sense, the opposite of the issue I'd had with Christian-based grimoires, which would happily reproduce various Hebrew words or even letters in a sort of mangled form that betrayed a fundamental lack of understanding of the alphabet or common divine names. The quest for authenticity has long been an issue in occulture, and for me personally, the grimoires that crippled the Hebrew alphabet in order to try to steal a little power from Jewish magic were like a marzipan apple. I hated seeing amulets where the Christian creator had been, for instance, unable to distinguish between the Hebrew letters yod (י) and waw (ו) and wrote down some deformed halfway thing instead.

Here was a grimoire that could have provided the authenticity missing from Christian grimoires, but it was denied by the translator himself, as if fitting in with stereotypical warnings against the practice of magic by certain rabbis. It made me think of old sci-fi movies where a voice-over informs us at the end that "there are some things that we are not meant to know."

I felt very disappointed. I considered that I had been "this close" to opening a door to some powerful magic only to find it locked by someone who should have been my ally. I closed the book and left it there.

Periodically over the years I would come across mentions of *The Sword of Moses* in the same translation, especially once the Internet came along. It was one of those things that people would sort of collect. I never found anyone who had actually used it (although other, much more popular grimoires, have suffered the same fate). I'd go and look at it again and feel the same disappointment and sense of loss. Here was a work that could be of value to modern magicians like me but that basically remained inaccessible. I had no idea then just how many more works of Jewish magic were out there in manuscript form that had never even gotten to the point of Gaster's bowdlerized version of *The Sword of Moses*.

Even after Joseph Peterson graciously added the transliterated divine names to Gaster's translation, I felt like the work was still out of reach. If Gaster had left out the divine names—or rather, shielded them from view, as there is a kind of reverse index of the names in the back of the original publication that gives the number(s) of the spells where the name occurs—what else might he have left out? By that time, I'd read about how, for instance, A. E. Waite, member of the Hermetic Order of the Golden Dawn, had tucked all sorts of his own stuff into his translations of alchemical works, so I just didn't trust the translation anymore.

For me, it took Yuval Harari's translation of *The Sword of Moses* from a completely different manuscript to pull me into the possibilities that *The Sword* presented for the modern magician. My main reason for hope was that Harari was a scholar instead of traditionally religious and so had no dog in the race; he clearly saw no necessity of hiding the divine names from profane eyes. But that translation didn't happen until 2012, and I didn't come across it until a few years later.

That sent me down a path of exploration and research that has led to this book. I wanted to bring *The Sword* into the present so that magicians might be able to actually use it and, in that way, not only enliven an old stream of magic but repay the nameless Jewish magician in northern Israel in the third quarter of the first millennium for their knowledge and their work in compiling all these spells, thank them for composing the ritual to enact them, and turn on the 1,800 divine names.

The Sword of Moses is written in a combination of Jewish Babylonian Aramaic and Hebrew and has three sections. The first section makes the argument that it is perfectly okay to adjure angels in order to do magic—and although this issue is not addressed in the work, it allows us to involve angels in cursework. (This absence indicates that the ethics involved must be all our own . . .) This is based on the story of Moses's own interaction with the angels when he went up to receive the Law on Mount Sinai. Just as the angels were forced to back down from challenging his validity for being there, so God obliged them for all time to assist all human beings who properly prepared to invoke them for magical purposes.

Having set up the rationale for why adjuration of heavenly spirits is fine, the author then outlines a three-day ritual that will purify the magician who wants to tackle adjuration. This ritual involves a modified type of fasting (you eat at night, only bread and water), ritual bathing, dressing in white clothing, saying the Standing Prayer three times per day, and the recitation of strings of divine names. We must be in a purified state in order to say the divine names, but our ritual purification must be complete in order to use the angels' power in spellwork. Otherwise, we endanger ourselves, as Hebrew angels are not the simpy creatures of Victorian spiritualists. They are fierce Fire spirits who are easily offended and perfectly happy to destroy people who dare approach them in a state of ritual impurity.

However, once we are ritually purified and we have adjured all the thirteen princes of the heavenly spirits—and thus have attained control over the spirits under them—we are ready to use the Sword—the 1,800 divine names—to do spellwork. I have to admire how the magician who wrote this book arranged the spells and attached to each one a string of divine names that give power to each spell individually. Most spells call for maybe five to ten names, although a few require quite a list. All the names are listed in order of use, so spell 15 starts at X and ends at Y, and spell 16 starts at Y and ends at Z. It is a model of the sort of efficiency that a good professional magician would need to conduct a thriving magical business and cut down on the sort of overwhelming information that many magicians face, even in ancient times.

The last section of *The Sword* is composed of 136 spells that run the gamut from curing headaches to death spells. None of these involve any particularly exotic *materia magica*; if the spell calls for some material, it can be something as simple as a pitcher of water or a bay leaf. This again emphasizes to me that *The Sword* was a real working magician's book, not a prop to sell to a nouveau riche merchant, like some of the medieval grimoires calling for exotic ingredients, fancy incenses, scented oils, and cool but spendy props like swords, knives, chalices, and so forth. You don't even need a wand with this book. Your weapon, your sword, is the divine names spoken by your own voice. Now that's empowering!

And the fact that this is so clearly a real, working book of magic that was regularly used by a professional magician is why I worked to make it available to you. I not only approached the translations but also went back to the original manuscript and did a good deal of research on the context of this work in order to understand it as fully as possible and thus to explain it clearly and make it a viable work that any committed magician can use today. I will not forget that day in the library when I saw that so inaccessible of a landscape. That place is here, now, for you to enter. I hope you will use it to make more magic in the world.

BACKGROUND OF
THE SWORD OF MOSES

When we talk about "early Jewish magic literature," we mean Jewish magic of late antiquity and the early Middle Ages, from *Sefer Ha-Razim* to the works in the Cairo Genizah.[1] *The Sword of Moses* (*Ḥarba de-Moshe*) and *Sefer ha-Razim* (*The Book of Secrets*) are the two Jewish books of magic that have come down to us from the first millennium. Other books of Jewish magic probably exist in uncatalogued works, especially as fragments (or even entire books) in the manuscripts found in the Cairo Genizah.* But right now, all we know about is *The Sword of Moses* and *Sefer ha-Razim. The Sword* is more significant than *Sefer ha-Razim* because it is "the broadest extant collection of Jewish magical recipes from the first millennium."[2]

---

* A *genizah* is a storage area for any documents that might include written divine names. If a book or manuscript containing divine names is damaged or becomes unusable, it is kept in a genizah until it is buried. The Cairo Genizah was located in the Ben Ezra synagogue in Old Cairo and received over 400,000 texts from 950 to 1250 CE. At some point it was walled up and forgotten. When the wall was removed in the eighteenth century, the trove of documents was discovered. The writings include everything from contracts to bills for labor to commentaries on the Hebrew Bible as well as mystical and magical documents, often in fragments or single pages. These manuscripts have all been removed, and most of them are in the libraries of Cambridge University, the Jewish Theological Seminary of America, and the Bodleian Library at the University of Oxford.

EARLIER FORMS OF JEWISH MAGIC

Qumran Exorcism Texts

The earliest examples of Jewish magical literature are from the Dead Sea Scrolls (also known as the Qumran Caves Scrolls).[3]* Texts regarding the exorcism of demons and how to protect oneself from them have been found in the Qumran Caves dating back to about 100 BCE. At least one of them makes magical use of Psalm 91 as a protective spell,[4] so we can see how long psalm magic, which is still popular today, has been practiced—more than 2,000 years.

Despite the command that we "shall not suffer a witch [the word used is actually *sorceress*] to live" (Exodus 22:18), no female witches are depicted in these earliest texts or in fact anywhere that I know of in Jewish magical texts of late antiquity.[5] Plenty of magicians are mentioned in all sorts of texts, but they are almost all men. Women who practice magic are mentioned in the Hebrew Bible, such as the Witch of Endor, although she is a necromancer rather than what we would now think of as a witch: someone who is more closely attuned to nature and who works directly with spirits rather than angels. We likewise don't come across mentions of women magicians like root-cutters, as in Greek magic, but that does not mean that witches didn't exist as part of ancient Jewish magical practice, only that written evidence of them has not been discovered so far. Personally, I

---

* The Qumran Caves were carved into the rock to be used as houses and storage areas by the people who once lived in the area of the Judean Desert on what is now the West Bank of Israel. They were discovered by local Bedouins to contain a number of Hebrew scrolls and fragments mainly from 300 BCE to 100 CE, but some from as far back as 800 BCE and as late as 1100 CE. Many of the texts are copies of Biblical texts but others are of non-Biblical books, like the *Book of Enoch* and the *Book of Jubilees*.

have often thought that witches were more often composing and providing incantation bowls because they are so closely associated with the home and the newly dead.

As mentioned, magical texts themselves do not mention sorceresses or female witches, but the rabbis do and explicitly connect them to women who are not under the control of men, such as old women, innkeepers, market vendors, and widows.[6]

Incantation Bowls

One very popular magical product was incantation bowls, which are cross-cultural, whereas *The Sword of Moses* is not especially so. These were simple conical clay bowls inside of which is a spiral of writing in Jewish Babylonian Aramaic. At the center is an image of a bound demon—frequently Lilith—usually depicted in chains and furthermore within a binding circle.[7] These bowls were used as protective devices by Jews and Gentiles in ancient Iran, Iraq, and Syria. The bowls were buried at the threshold of a home, at the corners, or in cemeteries and were intended to trap demons or malign spirits. Typically, they were created by Jewish magicians and other professional magic workers. To me it seems that at least sometimes these bowls were meant to protect the living from the restless dead: they are found in cemeteries and in the courtyards of homes where someone had recently died. It's also clear that sometimes they were used to focus demons on an enemy. Think of the cone of the bowl as a sort of megaphone that can be directed away from a house (to guard it) or toward the house (to curse it).

About two-thirds of these bowls date back to the beginning of the second millennium BCE in Mesopotamia—in other words, they occurred way earlier than *The Sword of Moses* or *Sefer ha-Razim*. They were generally buried on each side of a building's entry, under the doorway, or at the corners of one's house to protect against demons. A few were written on skulls.[8] It was a common belief that demons entered a house through the corners and the threshold.[9] Sometimes tar and cord were used to fasten two bowls together to make the protection especially powerful. Occasionally, bowls had a blank space for a name (I wonder if this worked as a sort of model that a magic worker would show a client: "I can make two of these for you"), but in this case, instead of it being used for the client, it indicated the client's enemies, from whom the bowl was meant to protect them. Leaving the enemy's name blank was one way of erasing or diminishing them.[10]

The texts of incantation bowls were often passed down from one generation to another, but it's clear that magicians-for-hire felt free to modify them;[11] Jewish magical practitioners of late antiquity didn't think they had to follow texts to the letter when it came to these bowls or to spells in general. As they could make bowls for Jews as well as Gentiles,[12] it seems that they could do magic for anyone, and that people of other cultures thought Jews were worth hiring as magic workers.

Even though incantation bowls are very much in the tradition of Jewish magic, they are a Jewish Babylonian device rather than a tool that arose in the Land of Israel like *The Sword* and like the magical texts from the Cairo Genizah.[13] They also have different magical goals than the Genizah magic texts. The bowls were meant to protect from demon-caused illness primarily, but they also helped the client attain social influence and favor with big shots, and a few were intended for cursing an enemy with pain and even death.[14] I think such devices would be very helpful for the contemporary witch, so consider looking into "incantation bowls."

The Sword of Moses is also quite different from the incantation bowls. The historiola "Swift Messenger," which is part of The Sword, appears on one of the incantation bowls, however.

Magic Texts from the Cairo Genizah

The magic of Genizah texts covers much wider goals than the bowls did. They advise how to perform healing, how to protect from venomous creatures, how to induce love or cause sexual attraction, cure spell-caused impotence, find treasure, discover a thief, win at trial or gain the favor of the authorities, enable a person to retain all learning, especially of the Torah—which was a coveted skill and brought respect and therefore social power and, which we will see, was important for a professional magician—and more.[15] In many ways The Sword of Moses has more in common with these texts than with the incantation bowls.

Sefer ha-Razim

Sefer ha-Razim is the oldest Jewish magic book that we know of,[16] probably dating to around 200–300 CE, which means it is older than even the Sefer Yetzirah, a mystical book often utilized in Jewish magic, which some date from 400 CE and others to 900s CE. (The Sword was composed sometime between these two dates.) The author of Sefer ha-Razim lived in the eastern Mediterranean in the late Roman or early Byzantine period. They knew Greco-Roman magic and astral magic well and integrated these with Jewish traditions.[17] By the beginning of the second millennium, this magic book was popular with Egyptian Jews.[18] It has survived over the centuries and is still used as a device to repel evil by some modern Jews.*

The *Sefer ha-Razim* that we know was compiled by Mordecai Margalioth in modern times, mostly from manuscript fragments culled from the Cairo Genizah. For that reason, some scholars don't believe that this book existed as a complete text in the first millennium; they think it was in bits and pieces even then.[19]

Sefer ha-Razim has seven chapters, which correspond to the Seven Heavens. These are similar to the setup of adjurational works like Hekhalot and Merkavah, but we can also see the influence of 1 and 2 Enoch.[20] The angels of each heaven in *Sefer ha-Razim* act independently of each other, which is reminiscent of the Hekhalot arrangement of angelic tiers or palaces; in comparison, the angels of each level in *The Sword of Moses* are dependent on angels higher up, with the top level commanding them all. The magical practice of *Sefer ha-Razim* is the adjuration of angels in order to gain the gift of prophecy, healing, hexing, or wealth.

The Sword of Moses also focuses on the adjuration of angels for magical purposes, but it does not have the Greek influence of *Sefer ha-Razim*. Compared to the complex spells and ingredients of *Sefer ha-Razim*, *The Sword of Moses* is a simple text.[21]

In adjuration, the magic worker, using the entity's name, calls upon a spirit or god to do some task. In Jewish magic, angels are traditionally called upon, since, as *The Sword of Moses* describes, YHVH gave us the right to command angels; we don't have the right to

---

* It's easy to find small, cheaply bound copies of this book intended to serve as protection devices, but they almost instantly fall apart if you try to study them, and the type is poor and even sometimes illegible. If you want something to study that contains both English and Hebrew, the only choice at this point is Margalioth's book, but there is a lot of controversy about this version of *Sefer ha-Razim*.

THE MAGIC OF THE SWORD OF MOSES

adjure God. This makes sense because, unlike with some other magical practices, the power to command spirits doesn't lie with us or even with the names of the spirits. That power has been granted to us by YHVH, who is the ultimate power. Adjuration is central in Jewish magical texts from Babylonia and the eastern Mediterranean in late antiquity and the early Islamic period.[22] Even magical objects from this time that are not books—like precious stones, magical jewelry, metal and clay amulets, and magic clay bowls in Babylonia—make use of adjuration: they ask a supernatural power to help someone.[23]

Hekhalot/Merkavah Magical Practices

Although there are a number of similarities between Hekhalot/Merkavah literature and the techniques of *The Sword of Moses,* practitioners of the former tended to use the rituals to become a teacher, be qualified to rule on questions of the law, determine if something or someone was ritually impure, and to identify thieves and murderers, gossips, and sorcerers.[24] This makes them sound more like they are filling the shoes of a rabbi rather than a magician; it is a more mainstream job, for the most part, than being a professional magician.[*] However, people who became experts in the practices of Hekhalot or Merkavah also acquired a measure of safety from attack, because the heavenly protection that came with such a position meant that anyone who attacked a "descender of the Chariot," as practitioners of Merkavah were called, would have great misfortune.[25]

Another indication of the age of *The Sword* is that it states that Moses was given gifts by the angels when he went up to receive the

---

[*] Even though in other times and places, a professional magician (or *ba'al shem*) was a community-sponsored position, for instance, in Jewish communities of Eastern Europe in the eighteenth and nineteenth centuries.

Law; this idea is mentioned in the Talmud (Shabbat 88b–89a). The method of purification is from this time period, and the Amidah prayer is used. The Amidah was composed during the time of the first synagogues that opposed themselves to the Temple rituals, substituting study for sacrificing animals or incense. This was from about 167 BCE to 70 CE. So the Amidah is older than *The Sword of Moses*. However, the structure of heaven and the names of the angels and the deity are right out of Hekhalot and Merkavah, two Jewish mystical (or perhaps magical) practices of earlier in the first millennium. Some[26] consider that just because *The Sword of Moses* has some similarities to magical practices that are part of Hekhalot and Merkavah, the author did not necessarily follow those methodologies; instead, perhaps both Hekhalot and *The Sword* pulled from an earlier practice that we don't know about. Lots of scraps of manuscripts exist from late Jewish antiquity, but most of them have not been translated, so currently we have no sure way of knowing about this. Also, it might be that their associated concepts were just prevalent in the author's society.

Rabbinic Magic

The branch of late antique Jewish magic that *The Sword of Moses* belongs to doesn't show connections to the Rabbinic stream. That is more common in the eastern branch of late antique Jewish magic.[27] However, the rabbis definitely used magic books, and we have proof of this, as I will discuss below. So the idea that the rabbis opposed magic and persecuted those who practiced it is incorrect. Nor were magical practices hidden or secret among Jews. And of course, no one was burned at the stake for practicing it. It was simply accepted.

THE HISTORY OF MAGICAL SWORDS
IN JEWISH MAGIC

There are others besides Moses who ascended to heaven and received magical words. One of these is Rabbi Akiva (50–135 CE), who is described in *Hekhalot Zutarti* as meditating on the vision of the Chariot—the heavenly throne as described in Ezekiel 10:14, which has traditionally been an image of meditation in Merkavah mysticism as well as later Jewish mysticism—and who received a name that enabled him and his students to accomplish magical acts.[28] He could bring down occult knowledge to work in the world without any disapproval from God.

In another magical work, *Sefer Shimmushei Torah* (*The Magical Uses of the Torah*), we hear how Moses ascended to heaven to get the Torah, but while there, he had confrontations with the angels, as we see elsewhere. However, in this work, Moses learns how to read the Torah as a magical text through the rearrangement of the words and letters into names that have magical potency. In this version, the "things" or "words" that the angels give him are *segulot*—magical remedies.[29]

However, one of the most profound conclusions I've come to from studying *The Sword of Moses* is how much the angels seem indeed to *be* God, in particular because of the recurrence of parts of the ineffable Tetragrammaton* in their names.

USING DIVINE NAMES

In the Hebrew Bible, we are told how, before he became a leader, Moses came across an Egyptian overseer who was beating a Hebrew

---

* The four-letter name of God, YHVH.

worker. We're told that Moses first looked both ways—which is something that seems so human to me—and then "slew" the Egyptian. I always imagined that he punched him to death. However, we get another version of this story in *Pirkei de-Rabbi Eliezer* (*Chapters of Rabbi Eliezer*), a rabbinic work written between the eighth and ninth centuries that includes commentary on various stories in the Hebrew Bible, the discussion of various customs (such as putting out the *havdalah* candle with wine and dotting one's eyelids with that wine), plus a section on astronomy, written in Aramaic in the Land of Israel.[30] Here's how the story is reframed in *Pirkei de-Rabbi Eliezer*: "Moses went into the camp of Israel, and saw one of the taskmasters of the Pharaoh smiting one of the sons of Kohath . . . He [Moses] began to curse him with the sword of his lips and he [Moses] slew him, and buried him in the midst of the camp . . . He went forth on the second day, and he saw two Hebrew men striving. He told him that [they were] acting wrongly: 'Why do you smite your fellow?' Dathan said to him: 'Do you wish to kill me with the sword of your mouth?'"[31] Whoever wrote this knew the tradition that Moses killed the Egyptian not by hitting him but by invoking the divine name. But here, instead of invoking the divine name, the writer says he curses the Egyptian with the sword of his mouth. This fits with the idea of the power of the sword of words in *The Sword of Moses*.[32]

Hekhalot Zutarti (*The Lesser Book of the Heavenly Palaces*), the oldest Hekhalot text, composed in Hebrew and Aramaic and probably written in the Land of Israel in the second or third century CE, contains the following: "This is a book of wisdom, understanding and knowledge, and inquires about (that which is) above and below, the hidden matters of the Torah and heaven and earth, and the mysteries (God) gave to Moses the son of Amram and he revealed to him at Horeb by which the world is sustained. And by it Moses performed the signs and wonders which he performed in Egypt, and by it he smote the Egyptian."[33] Two scholars[34] believe that the word *Horeb*, the name of a town, is a corruption of the Hebrew word for sword, *harba*, and that therefore the last sentence should read "and he revealed to him a sword by which the world is sustained. And by it Moses performed the signs and wonders which he performed in Egypt, and by it he smote the Egyptian."

In addition, in Rabbinics* it is said, "Let the high praises of God be in their mouth and a double-edged sword in their hand" (Ps. 149:6). The sword is interpreted as being the Torah itself,[35] which is not only composed of words but is an important aid to the magician in this period—and even today. This is why there are various rituals for attaining a complete knowledge of the Torah (the *Sar Torah*/ Prince of the Torah rituals). Such knowledge is what the Prince of the Torah grants; not only are the secret magical meanings of stories and phrases revealed, but the divine names—words of great power, which might be acronyms, for instance, and so not plainly visible to the ordinary person—are freely available to the magician for building magical phrases and words for spellwork of all sorts. Knowing the Torah very well, then, was an important magical skill at that time.[36]

The reciting of Torah (the mouth) is considered to be equal to wielding a sword in Rabbinics.[37] These examples show that the rabbis were acquainted with the idea that the Torah, especially when spoken or read aloud, could act as a sword, and that's where the

---

* Rabbinics is the name for mainstream Judaism during the period of the Talmud, or when oral Law came to be written down. So from about 300 to 600 CE.

writer of *The Sword of Moses* got the idea of compiling a book of divine names to be used for magic and which he called "sword."[38]

Some other interesting examples of magical swords connected with words exist prior to the creation of *The Sword of Moses*. For instance, if you recite the Shema in bed before you go to sleep—this bedtime prayer includes references to four angels, by the way—the rabbis say that it is as though you held a double-edged sword in your hand that keeps demons away. The prayer is identified with the Torah.[39] Further, a fragment of text from the Cairo Genizah describes how when there got to be a lot of demons in the world—who were born of Lilith in this text—God gave Methuselah permission to write the divine name on a sword that he used to kill 900,000 myriads of demons with one blow.[40] Moses also did magic with his rod, which had divine names on it, giving it magical power.[41]

THE IMPORTANCE OF WORDS IN JEWISH MAGIC

In Jewish magic, the means for causing change in the material world are words, which then become actions in themselves: "There are statements that, when suitably uttered in the appropriate circumstances by the appropriate person and with serious intention, can create by their very utterance a new state of affairs in the world."[42] An example of this would be the bride saying "I do" during a wedding ceremony. If someone sitting in the pews says "I do," they don't become married instead. And if the bride says "Hell, yeah" instead of "I do," the celebrant might well insist that she say the correct words even though "Hell, yeah" means essentially the same thing. Likewise, if the bride said "I do" to herself at a gas station, the words would not have the same transformative power; she would not become married there either.

So the right words said by the right person in the right place and time are necessary for a particular kind of action to occur. We see this in magic all the time. And this interdependence of words, time, place, and person is especially important in Jewish magic, where, for instance, the correct purification ritual to establish the correct time is necessary as well as the correct words. In science, some action brings about an effect; in Jewish magic, that action comes primarily through words. If we look ahead at the *Havdalah of Rabbi Akiva* (*Havdalah de-Rabbi Akiva*), that work turns the ordinary havdalah ritual into a magic ritual against demons and sorcery involving the purification ritual usual to havdalah (ritual washing of hands), the right person (a Jewish person who is able to say the blessings and the prayers), a right time (the ending of the Sabbath), and the right place (the magician's own home). I think it's important to note that if you can't do the purification ritual, you can't do the magic ritual. Luckily, the purification ritual demanded by *The Sword of Moses* is not so difficult or long, although it does take up three days of one's time.

The magical power of words in Hebrew magic can go back also to the public reading of the Torah, where the person who reads aloud from the scroll is audited by two people reading the text from books that show the vowels (while the scroll does not) and that indicate the phrasing and sentence endings (also absent from the scroll). They help if the reader gets confused and correct the reader if a mistake is made. Being a person who watches and corrects the Torah reader is a position of importance in Jewish services. A mistake in a Torah reading could lead to at most an error in the meaning of a sentence, but in Jewish magic, it could bring disaster, since the angels are highly dangerous and can easily destroy a human being. To make errors or read or say words sloppily in an adjuration in Jewish magic invites violence from the angel that one is trying to work with.[43] On the other hand, if spirits good or bad refuse to do what is asked of them in an adjuration, they will be beaten with iron rods, which is another way of saying beaten by the Four Mothers of the 12 Tribes (Bilhah, Rachel, Zilpah, and Leah). A manipulation of the first letters of their names creates an acronym that gives the Hebrew word *barzel*, which means iron, and which protects a woman giving birth and her baby when used in some fashion, in that iron repels spirits of any kind.[44] It's interesting that this is such a feminine protection and threat. This might point to much older practices.

Actions that occur through speech in ancient Jewish magic are not confined to human activity, which makes them quite different from pronouncing wedding vows. The universe was created through divine words, which are made up of divine letters. We see this most distinctly in the creation of the golem, which occurs most importantly by the writing of words in divine letters. Rabbi Judah Loew (1520–1609) didn't create a soul for the golem; however, through holy letters he created one and also took its life.[45] In ancient Jewish magic, one is speaking not to the congregation but to supernatural entities, the divine world. Very powerful stuff. If a magic ritual of late Jewish antiquity doesn't work, it's not because it can't work but because the magician did it wrong.[46] It depends not on social conditions, like a wedding, but on spiritual ones. It also doesn't depend on any social recognition of the magician; even though in many ways, the magician in late Jewish antiquity does play the role of a shaman, they don't have to do that for the magic to work. They only have to follow the directions. It's not about tradition (remember that *The*

Sword of Moses is not an esoteric or secret or even a forbidden text) or belonging to a lodge. It's the purity ritual that removes the magician from mundane life and the words they use that give them the power, which is granted by the Divine (not the devil or even the angels adjured).

Just as not everyone can be a bride, not everyone can be a practitioner of Jewish magic. Purification rituals not only pull the individual out of the mundane world and their own personal lives but also change them in a way that will enable them to carry out the adjurations successfully and therefore have success with the spells.[47]

Four main types of Jewish magic exist: harming, healing, love, and the acquisition of knowledge.[48] I'll return to these divisions in the spellwork section.

WHY IT'S OKAY TO ADJURE ANGELS

According to *The Sword of Moses* itself, Moses brought the Sword* of holy names down from Mount Sinai along with the tablets of the Law.[49]

The story about Moses receiving the gifts from the angel is a Rabbinic tradition mentioned in the Talmud (Shabbat 88b–89a), which indicates that the Rabbis saw it as permissible to do magic that involved the adjuration of angels.[50]

Various stories exist as to what happened when Moses was obtaining the tablets of the Ten Commandments. The story of Moses going up to heaven to receive the Commandments and interacting

---

* When I use *The Sword of Moses*, I am talking about the entire manuscript. When I use "the Sword," I am talking about the list of 1,800 divine names that forms the center of *The Sword of Moses* and the pieces of which function to power all the spells in the book.

negatively at first with the angels appears in various places, from the Talmud (Shabbat 88b–89a) to *Great Sections* (*Pesikta Rabbati*),[51] chapter 20, where an angel scolds Moses, saying, "You have come from a place of filth to a pure place. You, born of woman, what are you doing in a place of fire?"[52]

But Moses prevails against this attitude by pointing out that only beings who exist on the material plane can carry out the Commandments.[53] For instance, in Shabbat 88b, he responds to the scolding angels' "accusation" that he was born of woman by asking, "It is written, 'honor your father and mother.' Do you have mothers and fathers?" Because the angels cannot carry out the Commandments, they have no right to criticize him for being "filth"; he *can* be purified.

In the Talmud, we are told that God commanded the angels to obey humans who adjure them.[54] "Immediately, each and every one of the angels became an admirer of Moses and passed something to him, as it is stated: 'You ascended on high, you took a captive, you took gifts on account of man, and even among the rebellious also that the Holy One might dwell there'" (Psalms 68:19). The meaning of the verse is: In reward for the fact that they called you "man," you are not an angel, and the Torah is applicable to you, you took gifts from the angels. And even the Angel of Death gave him something, as Moses told Aaron how to stop the plague, as it is stated: "And he placed the incense, and he atoned for the people" (Numbers 17:12). And the verse says: "And he stood between the dead and the living, and the plague was stopped" (Numbers 17:13). If it were not that the Angel of Death told him this remedy, would he have known it?

One of the gifts that Moses got from the angels was the words that could be used to control them—the Sword itself. This makes

Moses the archetype of the Jewish magician,[55] although when you think about it, he had already proven his skill as a magician when he bested the Egyptian magicians in Pharaoh's palace.

In the various descriptions of how each angel gave Moses something, the word used is usually translated as "something" or "things" or more freely, as "gifts" (DVR in Hebrew) by which the world is run. In the context of magic, if we say that each angel gave Moses a word, then we can understand this to mean that each angel gave Moses a spell, since in Jewish magic, the word is the primary magical tool.[56] The angels gave Moses these words or spells because they saw that God gave Moses and the rest of us the Torah. The gift that God gave Moses was way bigger than what the angels gave him, but that act gave them not just permission to give him the words/spells they did but also approval to do so.[57]

Also, the fact that the angels give Moses these divine names means that while God is not directly involved in magic, magic can be empowered by God. In other words, magic is real and not forbidden; on the contrary, magic is fine with God, who has given us a way to practice it with power. At the same time, God does not become like the gods of the *Greek Magical Papyri*, for instance, whom the magical worker often directly addresses, commands, berates, and even threatens in case they don't perform particular magical works for the magician or even if they are slow about it.

THE HAVDALAH OF RABBI AKIVA

The Havdalah of Rabbi Akiva[58] is a combination of spells from Jewish Babylonia and the Land of Israel that we have in manuscript form from the fourteenth century but that most likely dates back to around the same time as *The Sword of Moses*. Havdalah, still done today, is a ritual that serves to separate the sacred time of the Jewish Sabbath from the mundane time of the rest of the week. It typically involves lighting candles and drinking a glass of wine. The purpose of this particular havdalah, though, is to protect the individual named in it from demons and curse magic, to help him if he is having sexual problems with his wife, to enable him to learn more easily and be more intelligent. Besides the candles and glass of wine, this havdalah calls for a full container of clean water to be present. The magician doing the work not only pronounces the ordinary havdalah service but also adjures powerful angels and holy letters of the Hebrew alphabet* to protect the client from sorcery, evil spirits, and injury, calls for expulsion of various demons, and reverses curses. A prince of forgetfulness is invoked to protect the client and help them with learning. Incantations contain divine names, verses from the Hebrew Bible, combinations of various Psalms, and magical prayers. When finished, the magician takes the water to the client that night to be used in a cleansing ritual.

THE SPELL-LOOSENER OF RABBI HANINA BEN DOSA (PISHRA DE-RABBI HANINA BEN DOSA)

Another magic book that came out at the same time is *The Spell-Loosener of Rabbi Hanina ben Dosa*. Rabbi Hanina ben Dosa was renowned as a miracle-worker who would effect miraculous healings and other acts through his prayers.

---

* A good example of how important writing is in Jewish magic.

CHARACTERISTICS OF JEWISH MAGICAL TEXTS

Jewish adjuration texts have eight features in common:

1. They identify themselves as adjurations.
2. They appeal to entities like angels, princes (of angels), names, letters, or demons, asking or demanding that they act according to the magician's will.
3. They address them as "I" (compare to prayers, which often use "we"; this is the work of individuals, not communities).
4. They use specific verbs from certain roots.
5. They make their requests "in the name of" divine names, the names of angels, or holy names made up of letters or taken from Biblical verses that describe God's power or actions.
6. They often use a hastening and/or threatening phrasing when addressing the angels.
7. They don't use please or thank you; they are commanding.
8. They mention the name of the client as well as the client's mother's name.[59]

WHO WROTE IT, WHEN, AND WHERE

At least one scholar dates *The Sword of Moses* to the Land of Israel in 750-1000 CE, partly due to the language; if it had been written in Babylon, the author would have just used Jewish Babylonian Aramaic throughout. Hebrew was being used only in the Land of Israel at that time. The first part of the book is written partly in Hebrew and partly in Jewish Babylonian Aramaic and describes the history of *The Sword* and the preparation necessary to use it.[1] By the time of the Fatamid Dynasty (909–1171 CE), knowledge of Aramaic shrank in the Land of Israel,[2] so it's very likely that *The Sword* was composed before the arrival of the Muslims. The Hebrew foundation of the book is the adjuration part (and also the directions in general).[3] The framework is in Hebrew, the recipes are in Jewish Babylonian Aramaic with bits and bobs of Hebrew, and "The Swift Messenger" section is in Aramaic.[4]

Also, *The Sword of Moses* seems to fit together with other Jewish magical texts that were created at that time: *Havdalah of Rabbi Akiva* and *The Spell-Loosener of Rabbi Hanina ben Dosa*.[5] Both of these works probably date from the third quarter of the first millennium, so from 500–750 CE.[6]

At least three versions of *The Sword of Moses* exist that we know of today, the most recent being the longest but also the most corrupt.[7] The earliest manuscript version of *The Sword of Moses* known to exist is from a lengthy compilation of magical texts known as *Sefer Shoshan Yesod ha-'Olam* (*The Book of the Rose, Foundation of the Universe*). This copy was made by Rabbi Yosef Tirshom in Greece or Turkey in 1500–1533.[8] However, this sheds no light on the time, place, or person who wrote *The Sword*. Tirshom simply added it to his 600-page-long compendium of Jewish magical manuscripts and formulas. Held in the Geneva Library as MS Geneve 145, *The Sword* shows up on pages 60–84 of that manuscript. The manuscript is in good condition and the handwriting therein is very clear.

The most popular translation of *The Sword* is not from *Sefer Shoshan Yesod ha-'Olam*, though. It was instead a manuscript that was collected by its translator, Moses Gaster.[9] This version—popularly available nowadays online—might have originally been based on the *Sefer Shoshan Yesod ha-'Olam*,[10] although Gaster thought the book originated in the third to fourth centuries.[11]

The other copies of *The Sword of Moses* are fragments from the Cairo Genizah—dating mostly from the eleventh and twelfth centuries, although one is from the tenth. Some of them don't include the Sword—the divine names—at all, but just scraps of it, like the ending words of each empowering bit. And remember these are copies and not the original, which is earlier.

One indication of the age of the original *The Sword of Moses* is that it was referred to by name by Rabbi Hai Gaon at the beginning of the eleventh century. In a letter, he describes several books of magic he knew of and used without success, and one of them is *The Sword of Moses*.[12] Since Hai Gaon was living in Babylon at the time (in Pumbedita, now Falluja in Iraq), *The Sword of Moses* must have been important in Babylonian magic.[13]

An interesting note is that Hai Gaon says that he and others tried to use these magic books for years but could not get them to work; Hai Gaon believes this is proof that they are garbage and not from God.[14,15] It does make one wonder why they kept trying if they could never get them to work after years of attempts. But here's a bit of a clue: Rav Hai Gaon also rejected the idea that those who engaged in Hekhalot or Merkavah actually left their body and ascended on high. Instead, he believed that they only did so "in their heart"—in their imagination.[16] Neither their soul nor their body ascended, from his perspective, and this became the more or less accepted point of view among the rabbis from about the tenth century onward.[17] But the thing is—if you don't believe that the sages could ascend on high through some kind of double or through a soul, if it's just in the imagination of those who ascend, then how can you have the faith necessary to successfully work magic as in *The Sword*?

The fact that Hai Gaon mentions *The Sword* then doesn't necessarily mean that *The Sword* was written at that time. It only proves it existed prior to that time—especially because it's clear that it is at least partly composed of fragments of other works.[18]

However, the other thing that's interesting about Hai Gaon's remarks with respect to these magic books is that they were clearly not some esoteric, secret works and not only the rabbis knew and used them.[19] So did ordinary people. In other words, there was no secret guild of magicians; instead, it appears magic workers were quite up front and provided a magic-for-hire service to their community—and did not have to fear condemnation for doing so. What's more, people even used *The Sword* as a protective device, much as *Sefer ha-Razim* was used—and still is in some quarters.[20]

LANGUAGE IN *THE SWORD OF MOSES*

One aspect of this work that helps date and locate its author is the fact that it's written in a combination of Hebrew and Jewish Babylonian Aramaic. This is not the same as the Aramaic in the Bible (such as the *Book of Daniel*) or that which was spoken in Galilee (Jewish Palestinian Aramaic). Instead, it's a kind of legal language used to write the Babylonian Talmud (Mishnaic Hebrew).* The spells are in Jewish Babylonian Aramaic with Hebrew words (Hebrew at this time indicates that it was written within a location in the Land of Israel). The opening section is in Hebrew, but two subsections—the Swift Messenger and some practical directions—are in Jewish Babylonian Aramaic.[21] The author used mostly Hebrew with bits of Jewish Babylonian Aramaic to knit everything together. One spell is in both Jewish Babylonian Aramaic and Greek; clearly the writer did not know Greek, or they would not have repeated it.[22]

The Sword of Moses does not contain the Greek terminology present in *Sefer ha-Razim* and instead has more words in common with medical formulas found in the Babylonian Talmud.[23] Only the longest and most corrupt version contains Jewish Babylonian Aramaic translations of terms from Greco-Roman magic from *Sefer ha-Razim*, which are simply transliterated instead of being translated, again showing that the author did not know what these meant.[24]

This lack of Greek terminology and the focus in terms of practitioners on predominately rural people, rather than on city-dwellers, indicate that *The Sword of Moses*'s place of origin is late antique Land of Israel, probably around 750 CE.[25]

---

* The Babylonian Talmud was composed between 300 and 600 CE by Jews in Babylon (Iraq). It retells discussions and arguments between rabbis about Jewish law and interpretations of the Bible, but also includes many stories. It has 2,711 folio-sized pages.

INFLUENCE OF GREEK MAGIC

A few bits of *The Sword* seem to indicate Greek borrowings, but these associations are debatable. For instance, the name Abrasax/Abraxas appears. Some scholars say this entity is of Jewish origin,[26] and it has been shown that Jewish influences are common in the *Greek Magical Papyri* instead of the influence always going in the other direction.[27]

Likewise, Helios appears, but instead of just being associated with the sun, as in *Sefer ha-Razim*, he will answer all questions and even bring you a woman, tasks normally not associated with Helios.[28] We get the feeling that the author is just throwing things out there with this name.

A formula from Greek magic texts, "semea kanteu kenteu konteu kerideu darungo lukunx," appears in a mangled sort of Hebrew transliteration.[29]

The only other connection that *The Sword of Moses* has with Greek magic is one phrase that is copied over again in Jewish Babylonian Aramaic. Harari says the author did not understand what he copied, but Gideon Bohak offers other examples.

The use of a poppet and of a magic circle are both so common in various cultures of the time that they cannot be said to be borrowings.[30]

RELATIONSHIP WITH EGYPTIAN MAGIC

On the other hand, the use of a piece of donkey meat in a spell to separate a couple comes from Egyptian magic, since Set, who separated Osiris from Isis, was depicted with a donkey head.[31] On the other hand, we do know that *The Sword of Moses* was known and copied in Egypt at the beginning of the second millennium, as it was found in the Cairo Genizah.[32] At that time, the text itself was used as an amulet; strips were torn from it, folded, and fitted into amulet containers to be worn.[33] There is no reason why folks could not do this now.

Still, it's clear that *The Sword of Moses* is to some extent a stand-alone text and peculiar to the Land of Israel in the late first millennium.

The concept of a sword consisting of a series of nonsensical words does turn up in a couple of other Jewish magical texts,[34] but the author of *The Sword* greatly expanded on that list and made it an entire practice.

GERMAN JEWISH MEDIEVAL USE OF MAGICAL TEXTS LIKE *THE SWORD*

The Ashkenazi Hasidim (no relationship to contemporary Hasidim other than both are Jewish) were great promoters of Hekhalot, but not much evidence exists that they used *The Sword of Moses*. However, they did have other magic books that came from late antiquity, like *Sefer ha-Malbush* (*The Book of the Garment*), which could have been brought to Italy by migrants at the turn of the first millennium and the beginning of the second and which later turned up in Germany, among the Ashkenazi Hasidim.[35] This is one explanation of how this group got their hands on Hekhalot and Merkavah texts centuries after they were written. And they not only preserved these texts but edited them as well. They also practiced various other types of magic, such as making a golem,[36] for which purpose they utilized the *Sefer Yetzirah*, which some say was composed at the same time as *The Sword*, but others say that it was written much earlier.

THE STRUCTURE OF *THE SWORD OF MOSES*

The Sword of Moses is composed of an introduction that explains why it's okay to do this magic (perhaps tacked on later after the spells were compiled),[1] an operation for preparing for working the Sword, the Sword itself (a mass of unintelligible names), and a list of about 140 spells (sometimes called formulas or recipes) for healing, harming, protection, love, wealth, influence with the authorities, and more.

PREPARATION THROUGH RITUAL PURIFICATION

The purification ritual in *The Sword of Moses* consists of bathing, not having nocturnal emissions, no contact with "unclean objects" (corpses, cemeteries, dead animals, swarming insects, semen, menstrual blood, and especially impure liquids[2]), eating only pure bread and salt—preferably bread magicians make themselves—and drinking only pure water. The magician is also to fast during the daytime for three days and only eat bread and salt and drink water after nightfall.

Purification rituals similar to this go back to ancient times in Judaism. Of course, the priests of the Jerusalem Temple had to practice a strict type of purification, but during the Second Temple Period (516 BCE to 70 CE), ordinary people who belonged to the Pharisee sect began to practice ritual purification for their own purposes.[3] At this time, prayer and the public reading of the Torah in non-Temple spaces was on the rise, and those among the Pharisees wanted to make themselves ritually pure for these actions.[4] Ritual bathing in a mikvah* was involved, and sometimes mikvahs were attached to synagogues precisely for purification before prayer or Torah reading.[5]

Many who wanted to engage in public prayer or study not only purified themselves by washing but also became concerned about the ritual purity of food. The problem was that people who were ritually impure could "contaminate" food or even vessels for eating, like cooking pots and dishes, and that meant that the ritually purified person couldn't eat with others. To get around this, people used stone vessels, the same as what had been used in the Temple by the priests, especially for the ultimate purification ritual known as the Red Heifer, because stone cannot pass on impurity according to Jewish law. People were especially concerned about keeping foods in the classes associated with the Temple service pure, so meat and even ordinary food that had not been part of the sacrificial cult, like bread, were kept pure by using stone vessels. This allowed ritually pure and impure people to share food without a problem.[6] Some laws about ritual purity said that a person who purified themselves in a ritual bath would not be completely pure until nightfall.[7] This fits well with the practice of *The Sword* of not eating until after nightfall.

Historically, seeking ritual purity above and beyond what was necessary for ordinary people (as opposed to priests, while the Temple was still standing) was a way to attain holiness.[8] We can see this as part of the rise of individualism; ritual purity morphs from something only for priests—a class of people determined by forces beyond

---

* A *mikvah* is a body of water used for ritual purification. It should be water that is "living"—e.g., fed by a spring, a river, or the ocean. If your home water comes from a spring-fed reservoir, that will work. Most Jewish communities have a specially built place for ritual bathing.

THE MAGIC OF THE SWORD OF MOSES

individualism (inheritance)—to something anyone can do. And they don't need the Temple to do it, which was an especially important point once the Temple had been destroyed. Many lost faith in the religious authorities after that happened, and so they sought a much more personal and attainable sacredness.[9] People could attain ritual purity themselves by relatively simple means: bathing, eating pure foods, and using dishes that could not be made impure.[10] No fancy props or ashes of a red heifer were necessary.

The other side of this is that individual Pharisees who wanted to shift the focus away from the hereditary priesthood and the Temple authority could point to their own ritual purity as something that distinguished them from common people—although common people were also doing this, just not very many.[11] Holy people came to be more important than holy places due to practices like this. Most important for us, magicians came to use these methods of ritual purification in order to prepare for magic work during the Hellenistic period.[12]

Even so, this purification method was not from Greek practice and didn't contain the Greek or Christian concept of the body being lesser than the soul or of the soul being trapped in the (filthy) body. Jews considered the body as just as sacred as the soul, since it had been created by God and was therefore perfect.

This purification ritual is also similar to those that were a part of Hekhalot practices. Harari has argued that Hekhalot, Merkavah, and *The Sword of Moses* derive from a common ancestor, rather than *The Sword of Moses* deriving from Hekhalot itself. That might be true, but whether it is or not, an examination of the purification rituals for Hekhalot and Merkavah can be enlightening with respect to the purification ritual demanded in *The Sword of Moses*.

Many connections exist between Hekhalot practices and magical ones,[13] and these connections are more than the fact that both use magical names and similar techniques.

Hai Gaon, the eleventh-century Babylonian rabbi, also known as Hai ben Sherira, describes the technique of fasting for forty days (during the daytime, as in *The Sword*), sitting with his head between his knees (the Elijah position),* and whispering specified songs and praises to the ground.[14] He says that this is how one descends to the Merkavah—has a vision of the divine Chariot. The problem is that he gets the information from a text that's not describing how to see the Chariot but instead tells how someone would go about ensuring that one's life was preserved for the year following Yom Kippur. That day is even now sometimes considered the day when God decides who will live and who will not live through the following year.

The difference between the more ancient non-priestly purity practice and Hekhalot purification is that, for the latter, purification doesn't lead to any permanent state of spiritual perfection but only prepares the worker for an extraordinary event.[15]

So fasting in Hekhalot is not especially or even outright prescribed for attaining the vision of the Merkavah. Instead, fasting, ritual bathing, and abstaining from various things are preparation to say the divine names in order to conjure angels who will grant the operator boons, as in the Sar Torah practice;[16] we see this in *The Sword*. This kind of purification extends in Hekhalot to even more magical practices, like reviving the dead and divination through dreams,[17] which also involve the use of divine names. Some scholars even believe that Hekhalot was first about magic—the adjuration

---

* He sits with his head between his knees so he doesn't faint, not in order to make use of some physiological aspect of sitting in this way to produce hallucinations. S142.

THE MAGIC OF THE SWORD OF MOSES

of angels to receive boons through the use of divine names—and only later about mystical vision like seeing the divine throne.[18] What makes these rituals work is the use of the divine names, and that's why the purification is required.[19] Similar practices for the wielding of divine names occur in the Talmud.[20]

Fasting is very important in these rituals, whether they are in the Hekhalot or purely magical texts or in the Talmud, but most of the time these are partial fasts or fasts that restrict specific foods. Usually the fasting occurs only in the daytime. Often one must only eat bread prepared with one's own hands. The most common length of time for fasting is three days (the length of time the Israelites had to prepare in order to receive the Ten Commandments; see Exodus 19:15) or forty days (corresponding to how long Moses was up on Mount Sinai).[21]

Fasting was important in ancient Judaism, whether while preparing for and experiencing Yom Kippur or during mourning, which specifically forbade any activities that might be considered joyful, like eating meat, drinking wine, or having sex.[22] But some used fasting for sorcerous ends, such as those mentioned in the Talmud who went to a graveyard and fasted in order to see the deceased Rav Hiyya in a dream (Kil. 9:4 (32b)) or people who fasted in order that an "unclean spirit" might possess them (Sanhedrin 65b).[23]

In *Sar Torah* and in the "Incantation for the Great Name," certain foods were forbidden during the preparation time: meat, fish, and anything that produces blood.[24] Likewise, all vegetables were forbidden, which included onions, garlic, or garden vegetables. This might be because "wet" food can more easily be made impure than "dry" foods like beans—which the prophet Daniel ate to prepare for dream divination. It might be because of the body odors onions and garlic potentially cause—these rituals often stipulate avoiding smells[25]—but also perhaps because these were precisely the foods the Israelites cried about missing from their stay in Egypt when they were wandering in the desert.[26]

Oddly enough, Sar Torah rituals can involve drinking wine, such as some texts that prescribe certain names be written on leaves, dissolving the names in wine in a silver cup, sometimes while chanting incantations, and then drinking the wine.[27]

Eating bread made by one's own hands better enables the isolation that these rituals often prescribe.[28] For instance, in the Sar Torah operations in subsection 299 of *Hekhalot Rabbati*, the operator has to sleep alone in a room or attic for twelve days, and in the "Chapter of Rabbi Nehuniah ben ha-Qannah," he has to sit in a dark house.[29]

Hekhalot purity is not about attaining a permanent state of spiritual perfection but rather is a preparation for an extraordinary event.[30] In scholarship about Merkavah, fasting, ritual bathing, and seclusion have been treated as if they somehow create the state of ecstasy[31] or as if dietary restrictions have an effect on the practitioner's physical strength or consciousness.[32]

The idea of not looking at others doesn't seem to fit with the idea of becoming impure by doing so, since the rabbis ruled over and over that a person could not become ritually impure by looking at something or someone.[33] On the one hand, it is considered in this context that angels are very sensitive to the pollutions of the material world and are furthermore easily provoked. Still, these practices might be an outgrowth of folk beliefs.[34]

The other possibility is that perhaps this is more about distraction, since the idea of white clothes is at least partially so that a person won't be distracted by colored fabric.[35]

THE MAGIC OF THE SWORD OF MOSES

In terms of washing, for these rituals for Sar Torah, etc., not just the person must be washed but also their clothes, and sometimes this washing has to occur in a river.[36] This is clearly connected to the rule that a person can purify themselves ritually only in "living waters," of which a river is a great example.

On the other hand, the would-be conjurer of angels sometimes has to be careful about becoming in a sense *too* pure. For instance, in *Ma'aseh Merkavah*[37] (section 562), the Sar Torah operator has to stand inside a circle after purification so that demons don't mistake him for an angel and kill him.[38] This for me raises questions about the widespread practice of standing inside a circle when raising demons. It implies that if we did not engage in such purification, demons would not attack us—although our operation also wouldn't work, since the angels wouldn't heed a call from someone impure or, worse, they might become enraged at our hubris and kill us.* But it does make me wonder if some of the use of circles when calling on demons might not arise from the idea of the operator having purified themselves into a tempting morsel for demons.

With Hekhalot, asceticism is not about negating the material world but rather a means of gaining power,[39] and the type of asceticism found in *The Sword of Moses* is not Greek or Egyptian but Jewish.[40] In Hekhalot, it's assumed that the practitioner is already abstaining from sex, and it's not women who are impure but semen.[41] So the practitioner is advised not to have an accidental emission, even at night during dream, and this prohibition is probably especially important in Merkavah, since some of the work in

---

* Swartz, "'Like the Minister Angels,'" 162. Jewish angels are nothing like simpy Victorian angels. They would just as soon kill you as look at you. And this is considered in this context an indication of the high level of holiness of the Divine. It's not even personal. Rules of purity are higher in heaven than here on earth.

that practice involves dreaming. This stricture against emissions puts Hekhalot-style purification closer to practices described in Qumran texts than restrictions in Rabbinic Judaism such as the Mishnah and Talmud.[42] Qumran texts say outright that impure men have to stay away from pure angels lest those men be destroyed.[43] Interestingly enough, most of the rules about avoiding women in Hekhalot purifications—and only half of the rules mention doing this—don't mention menstruation or give any other reason, and at least one purification says men should be avoided as well.[44] This implies that maybe the issue with being around women or men is about getting distracted from the work rather than about impurity. If you want to invoke the Sar ha Torah, a powerful angel who could give you the knowledge of the Torah, you are told not to look at anyone at all, much less interact with them.[45]

The individual who wants to adjure angels in Hekhalot/Merkavah is advised to bake their bread themselves rather than eat bread baked by a woman. This seems not to be a purity issue, as the law was that a menstruating woman was freed from chores and from sex during her period, so she wouldn't be baking bread then anyhow.[46] Perhaps having a woman bake your bread might result in arousal, but in my opinion, being responsible for baking your own bread during a purification ritual focuses the magician more narrowly on the rite itself and also allows them to imbue the bread with their own intentions. I think this is especially important because the only thing the magician is allowed to eat in either *The Sword of Moses* or Hekhalot is bread and salt and water, and these only after sundown. This is quite different from Greco-Egyptian purification rituals for magic; they usually forbid only meat and wine.[47] The Hekhalot purification forbids eating vegetables, which might be because some of them cause gas or come out in one's sweat, and this would offend angels. I found this reasoning to be similar to Amazonian magicians who also follow a strict diet before working with spirits because the spirits think humans smell bad and won't heed the magician's call in that case.

In terms of ritual immersions in water—usually described as flowing, so river yes, pond no—the Sar ha Torah adjuration requires twenty-four immersions per day.[48] This means dunking one's head beneath the surface of the water rather than individual baths.

The length of time for the purification is also different in both Hekhalot/Merkavah and *The Sword of Moses* and also hearkens back to important time periods in Judaism: three days, seven days, twelve days, forty days. For instance, the three-day fast in Hekhalot before dreamwork might go back to the three days men were asked to purify themselves before the revelation of the Law at Mount Sinai.[49] This is quite different from the length of purifications in Greco-Egyptian magic, which is usually three to seven days.[50]

An interesting connection between a Sar ha Torah ritual and the Abramelin Operation is that the practitioner is advised to lock themselves in a room or attic for that time.[51]

It's notable that the purification that is asked for in Hekhalot/Merkavah and *The Sword of Moses* is transient. The practitioner is not thereby turned into a member of a sect or group. The purification rituals of Hekhalot, Merkavah, and *The Sword of Moses* also have in common that they are not communal undertakings.[52] They are personal, and that coincides with Harari's definition of one of the distinctions between magic and religious ritual—that magic is done by an individual and religion is more often a communal activity.

What's more, as in Hekhalot, the purity that is part of *The Sword* is not about attaining a permanent state of spiritual perfection but is instead preparation for an extraordinary event.[53]

PREPARATION THROUGH PRAYER

The prayer focused on in *The Sword of Moses* is the Amidah or the Standing Prayer. This is recited three times a day at the times that sacrifices of animals, grains, or incense were once offered in the Temple; the Amidah became the substitute for the Sacrificial Cult after the Romans destroyed the Temple of Jerusalem. It is still recited today as the main prayer of the Jewish liturgy (outside of the Shema). It was written by the Pharisees, who created synagogues as first a kind of competitor to the rigorously controlled Temple and its power by inheritance and later a substitute for the Sacrificial Cult after the Temple was destroyed by the Romans in 70 CE. Those in charge of the Temple were the Sadducees. The priests and Levites who ran the Temple had those offices because they inherited them. The Pharisees represented a non-inherited power center led by ordinary people who studied the Torah and became experts in it. So to a certain extent, the Pharisees were democratizers of Judaism. Also, the Temple rituals required people to buy the sacrifices and turn over a certain portion to the priests; the Pharisees didn't require payment other than help to maintain the synagogue—originally seen as a study house—just like any organization. There was also a lot of resentment among ordinary people against the priests and Levites, who were of the elite. Many ordinary people preferred worshipping in Pharisaic synagogues instead of giving money to the hereditary priesthood. Furthermore, the Pharisees resisted the Hellenization of Judaism, while the Sadducees did not. Right away, you know that the Sadducees were more educated, sophisticated—and powerful. They recognized only the written Torah and Greek philosophy as binding; the Pharisees rejected Greek philosophy, recognized Oral Torah (knowledge passed down orally), other books of the Bible besides the five main ones, and believed in the resurrection of the dead. The Pharisees went on to become the rabbis of Rabbinic Judaism, which continues to this day.

The Sword of Moses is outside of both parties and an even stronger democratizer of power, putting it in the hands of the ordinary person instead of a rabbi, much less a hereditary Jewish priest. If you think about that, you can see how attractive *The Sword of Moses* would be—not only did it offer a work-around to rabbinic power, but an ordinary person could, with the approval of God, command angels. This goes beyond other magical practices of, for instance, working with an angelic prince to acquire knowledge of the Torah and therefore set oneself up as an authority equal to the rabbis—and to gain influence in one's society among the people.

The Sword of Moses instructs the magician to recite the Amidah but also to incorporate two extra prayers: one asking God to bind the angels and one asking for protection from them. Then the angels themselves are adjured from lowest to highest level. Together with the Amidah, which is said three times daily, we are asked to do the adjurations of the thirteen princes, plus two prayers of adjuration that address God. One asks the Divine to bind the heavenly princes to the magician, and the other asks God for protection so that the magician is not burned up by the angels who are adjured.[54]

THE HISTORIOLA

One of the parts of *The Sword of Moses* text is an odd section called a *historiola*. Historiolae are relatively short texts that are incorporated into a magical spell.[55] One example we know of comes from Enuma Elish, the Babylonian creation story. The god Ea offered every living thing apricots and figs to eat, but the worm refused these good things and instead said it preferred to eat bones and flesh. Ea curses the worm and the story is followed by how one might treat a toothache magically.* This historiola gives an example from mythology of how a worm was cursed by a god; the spell that follows it tells how a magician can defeat a toothache-causing worm.

A historiola uses the past tense to indicate that what it describes happened in mythic time.[56] It brings forward something from the past in order to make use of its power. This fits very well with the story of Moses bringing down a gift from the angels—the Sword. At the same time, it is not so much that a link is created between the past and present with a historiola but that the past event has been completed, just as the desire is that the present practical problem should be "completed" in the sense that it be resolved.

A historiola doesn't necessarily have to end with a spell because it is itself a spell in story form.[57] Ancient Egyptians, who mostly could not read hieroglyphics, activated this kind of spell by either pouring water on a section of a stele written over with the hieroglyphics that formed the historiola or just touching that section.[58] I

---

* The idea that a worm causes a toothache would be familiar to witches who have worked with henbane; its toothlike calyxes indicate its magical usefulness against the worm believed to cause toothache. The herb was burned and the smoke funneled onto the cavity, the hole of the worm causing the pain in the tooth. The henbane smoke would kill the worm. Easy peasy!

think this shows very interesting possibilities for working with not only the historiola in *The Sword of Moses* but even the divine names through simply touching them. It is worth investigating whether merely touching, for instance, written parts of the Sword can activate magical spells.

Historiolae have three parts: a mythic dimension, a practical problem that needs solving, and the act of speech itself that is the remedy. They are most often connected with healing rather than cursing. A good example of a very short one—one of many from early Christianity—is a Coptic amulet against snakebite:

> Christ was born on the 19th of Choiak.
> He came descending upon the earth.
> He passed judgment on all the poisonous serpents.[59]

It is as if naming and situating the god and describing his descent and his actions when he got here are equivalent to that god performing that service now, as the historiola is spoken. The historiola can stand in for the words of a spell; it works as a spell itself.[60] It can also explain why a particular object or substance is used in the spell that follows.[61] And it can give a genealogy for a spell, its first use, or a description of how it came about.[62]

Something especially interesting in my opinion is that a historiola is meant to be taken as if it were said aloud even though it is written.[63] In a society where most people can't read, writing itself is power and embodies power, much as with, for instance, the incantation bowls or written amulets of the time.

Some historiolae gave the magician the opportunity to take the place of a god by using the construction "I am . . ."[64]

Sometimes the client's name is even included in the historiola, just as we might see in grimoires that leave a space for a name in a spell or ritual—"N son of N," as if inserting the client into mythic time or time completed.[65]

However, a historiola can even tell a mythical story that does not occur in any standardized story and is instead drawn from the whole worldview of the society that produced it and/or uses it to make magic. So, for instance, one historiola describes Jesus standing on the shore of the ocean and seeing Migraine coming out of the water with a lot of thrashing. Jesus asks Migraine what it is doing, and a conversation ensues, at the end of which Jesus not only tells Migraine to go away but specifies a person's name in real time (N son of N).[66] So a historiola uses a worldview as a sort of treasure house from which to create a myth for that time and space that will make magic.[67] It is worth considering how this might be done now.

Magic workers of both Babylonia and the Land of Israel used historiolae, which indicates that these two areas both populated by Jews shared magical techniques and devices.

THE SWORD ITSELF

What is different about this magic book compared to others is the enormous list of magical names that are then sliced up into groups to be used for each spell. The author combined and edited several lists of magic formulas, holy names, and fragments of incantations to create this work.[68] It looks like he grabbed some texts from amulets as well.

The book describes four levels of thirteen princes.

When the highest prince is adjured, not only that prince but also everyone below him is subject to the magician's authority.[69] Even so, *The Sword of Moses* recommends beginning at the bottom of the tiers of princes and working one's way up, which reminds me of how one works the Palaces in Hekhalot.* It's as if we need the practice on the less powerful angels in order to manage the most powerful ones.

Just as Moses did, the lowest four princes have authority over the Sword (the list of holy names) as well as over the Torah (the Hebrew Bible, especially the first five books) itself. This statement links *The Sword of Moses* and the Torah in terms of authority; the names of the Sword are from the mouth of God just as the words of the Torah are. Pretty big guns. In other words, the magician is able to work magic not because of the magician's own power but through the divine power that Moses received. These names hold this power as an honor to God. Again, we are not working with random or lesser spirits.

The idea that *The Sword of Moses* is connected to and therefore vetted and authorized by the Torah might be a response to the occasional condemnation of magic by the Rabbinic† stream of Judaism— at least, if people other than rabbis were doing it. In modern times, we are told that it was okay for the sages of old to do magic, because they were holy; it's not okay for us ordinary people. Hmm . . .

---

* These are the Seven Palaces of Heaven through which a practitioner of Hekhalot must travel in order to achieve the vision of heaven and of God. Each Palace is guarded by fierce angels who must be shown a special "seal" before they will allow the practitioner to pass through. Otherwise, they will just kill the person.

† Rabbinic Judaism began with the Pharisees, who opposed the monopoly of the hereditary priesthood of the Temple of Jerusalem and set up places for the study of sacred texts. This was a democratizing trend in Judaism and became the main practice after the Temple was destroyed by the Romans and the Talmud was transferred from oral to written form.

To gain control of the Sword, we are told to perform in secret a three-day ritual of purification, prayer, and adjuration. The writer's directions about how to attain control over the Sword are purely their own; these instructions were not copied from anywhere else, even though they share some things in common with other texts.[70] This once again demonstrates that magicians of the past were not afraid to come up with their own techniques.

Although it was originally shorter,[71] the Sword itself consists of 1,800 names and includes three short texts (like a sentence) that are taken as names.[72] These names are compiled from various magical formulas but not from Greek magical texts; the author of *The Sword of Moses* did not know Greek. The words of the Sword are not acronyms either; they are meaningless—and that's for a very good reason: human beings cannot speak the language of angels. And the opposite is also true, to some extent; in *Sota* 33a, the Talmud says that the angels don't pay any attention to personal requests made to the angels in Aramaic because they don't speak Aramaic. On the other hand, Rashi (1040–1105), widely considered the foremost commentator on the Torah and Talmud, advised people to use Aramaic in some prayers in order to keep away demons, because they don't understand Aramaic either.[73] I wonder if he was responding to amulets inviting demons to come and eat because since they can't eat, asking them to participate in such functions is a way to get rid of them.[74]

The Sword also contains a few Jewish Babylonian Aramaic sentences.[75] Each section of names averages about ten words, which makes me wonder if there is any numeric significance.[76]

The names are used to empower almost 140 spells, which constitute the third part of *The Sword of Moses*. Some spells use the same names as others. The first two spells are pretty wide-ranging; the rest are generally more specific. Some spells include directions for reversing them. From the sheer breadth of the situations the spells cover, the magician clearly provided a wide range of services to their community: healing, cursing, causing someone to fall in love with or have sex with the client, spells to bring success in agriculture or trade or for releasing someone from prison, divination, and exorcisms (the oldest known type of Jewish magic, dating back to Qumran).

This raises the shamanic aspect of *The Sword of Moses*. Magicians might not have been born with a caul or in some other way have indicated they were chosen for such work by visions or retreat or whatever, but the magicians removed themselves from their community to do the ritual (done in secret), purified themselves through seclusion, fasting, and praying, and then had contact with the spirits who gave them powers that they could then use to do works for their community. This seems to meet the definition of shamanism.

Writing the Divine Names in The Sword

Ma'aseh Merkavah (*The Work of the Chariot*) describes writing on oneself the "seals," i.e., the divine names, which serve to protect the operator from the dangers of angels. For example, "By the Seven Seals that Rabbi Ishmael sealed on his heart. 'WRYS SSTYY' on my feet, 'BG BGG' on my heart, 'RYS TYP' on my right arm, 'WRYS TSY Y'H' on my left arm . . . (etc.)."[77] This means that there is a tradition of writing the names on one's body, which reminds me of how divine names are written on the clay body of a golem in order to animate it. In this case, though, the names are written in order to protect the magic worker from the wrath of angels, who can be easily offended by humans.

This practice of writing the names and basically wearing them is outlined in *Sefer ha-Malbush* (*The Book of the Garment*), possibly written in the sixth to eleventh centuries,[78] which means it could be contemporary with *The Sword of Moses*. It is often found in *Sefer Raziel ha-Malakh* (*The Book of Raziel the Angel*), which was compiled from various magical texts around 1100 CE. However, *Sefer ha-Malbush* was apparently written in Babylonia rather than in the Land of Israel. This book, only a few pages long (folio pages 2b–7a in *Sefer Raziel ha-Malakh*), describes making a sort of hooded poncho out of strips of parchment woven together. Divine names are written on the garment. (I'm thinking since it's woven of strips, the names would be written on the strips before weaving them together—that would certainly make it easier.) An especially long string of names is to be written around the hood—or even on a gold wreath worn instead of a hood. Then, after seven days of fasting in the daytime and breaking the fast only with vegetables and nothing from animals, not even eggs, the magic worker wears it to some living waters and receives a sign as to whether they are pure enough to proceed with adjuring angels. If they get the go-ahead by the appearance of a clear red light shining above the water, the magic worker wears the garment into water up to their waist and can adjure various angels, who will accompany the magic worker and do their will for up to four hours. Among other things, upon coming out of the water, the magician is taken for an army by anyone who sees them. This can be repeated for seven days, getting four hours of magical power each day.

However, the *Sefer ha-Malbush* is not the only work possibly from the same time period as *The Sword of Moses* that makes a connection between the divine names and the person. A case can be made that seals described in the Hekhalot of the operator presenting to the angels of each of the seven palaces for protection and permission to enter would have been written on the individual's body, not on some object or even on their clothing.[79] When I read the descriptions in Hekhalot and Merkavah about the seals, I must admit I wondered what they were written on. First, there's the issue of ascension. If you literally rise to the Palaces—which is the assumption before we get to revisionists like Rav Hai Gaon, who says ascension to the Palaces is all in the practitioner's mind (or "heart")—then the question is whether the operator actually leaves their body or creates a double or makes use of a particular piece of their soul, etc. If they do not rise physically—and most of the stories about witnesses to this kind of ascension practice describe seeing the body of the practitioner present but the person absent (very similar to descriptions of witches who flew to the Sabbat, leaving behind their body as if in a coma—then it would not be possible for the person to carry any sort of material seal. Perhaps marking the seals literally on the body with ink would mean that those seals would be carried aloft with the duplicate of the body and thus guarantee their usability once the practitioner got to the Palaces.

I also wondered if the seals might be tattoos. This would provide protection forever and is *not* forbidden by the Hebrew Bible, which only disallows tattoos made to honor other gods rather than tattoos in general. This would certainly make things easier for the practitioner.

And such a practice—literally writing names on the body—also coincides with the use of names to enliven the body of the golem. During that operation, names are written on the various limbs to enliven them, with the caution that the operator not misspell them or write them on the wrong limb or area, since then they would themselves become disarranged and perhaps die or at least be greatly damaged. The implication is that writing on a clay body is like writing on one's own body and comes with great powers.

However, if we do decide to write these names upon our own body, whether with ink or in other ways, then the same caution as mentioned for the golem applies even more. Be very careful of the spelling!

One possibility to consider is writing the names on the prayer shawl or even on a so-called *tallit katan*, which is traditionally worn under the clothing and which furthermore has a shape very similar to the garment described in *Sefer ha-Malbush*: a kind of a poncho, although it does not have a hood. A tallit katan is cheap and easy to get online.

If you wear a dress, you can always convert a slip to a four-cornered garment by cutting a slit in each side seam. Then make a hole in each of the four corners of the slip and tie ritual fringes (tzitzit) on them. You can buy the fringes already tied or tie them yourself. You can then write the divine names on that garment. You could actually do something similar with a T-shirt. The point is that it has to have some resemblance to a four-cornered garment, so leaving the side open up to the waist is considered fine. For a slip, you could use a full slip and cut the seams up to the hips and attach the tzitzit to the corners.

THE SPELLS

The spell section begins with lots of healing spells that start with illnesses of the head and go down to the feet; this was a common order not only for Greek medicine but also for Babylonian.[80] Later spells deal with farming issues, falling into a well, and so forth, and no spells deal with conducting wars or dealing with princes, as the Greek-associated spellbooks might well do.[81] Just as the divine names were the product of the writer's editing, so were the spells.[82] While today, a current in occulture states that in order for magic to work, one has to follow grimoire formulas *exactly*, in the many magical scraps from the Cairo Genizah we see slavish exactness was not a thing in Jewish magical practice.[83] Not only did a spell vary from one magic worker to another, but the same spell could be constructed in various ways by the same practitioner. The compilation of spells in *The Sword* is probably also the result of magical knowledge being passed down—or shared or borrowed—rather than just the writer creating it all.[84]

Treating the Sections of The Sword like Talismans

The Sword itself, a mass of 1,800 names, includes groups of names, for instance, that include YH or EL, names that come before S(Ts) B'WT, names that are alphabetized, and names that are N son of N.[85] So it's apparent that the writer took a lot of care arranging these names. They are not just a jumble. And the writer did not just make them up; there are too many similarities in words used in amulets from around the same period and the divine names in the Sword.

Something especially interesting to me is the possible connection with amulets from previous times. When I first examined the divine names in The Sword, I noticed there were a lot of repetitions and reversals. These struck me first as perhaps remnants of an oral tradition, something like what I noticed when I became a Torah reader for my synagogue and observed the kind of letter and sound repetitions that would be handy for reciting and recalling an oral text—and we know that the Five Books of Moses, i.e., the Hebrew Bible, had an oral existence before they were set down.[86] I concluded that it would be appropriate to arrange the divine names for each spell in talismanic form, emphasizing repetition and placement graphically. This would make them more sigil-like and, in my opinion, easier not only to focus on but also to imbue with magical intention.

Oddly enough, when I came across information about the various magical amulets found in the Cairo Genizah, one scholar pointed out how many qualities of an oral text these had—such as formulaic phrases, repetition, and rhythmic patterns—that implied that they had been chanted out loud.[87] When I saw some of the reproductions of these devices, I was struck by how some repetitions were similar to those in *The Sword*, such as the repetition of *YodHey*. What's more, some have found parallels between amulets and magical texts in the Cairo Genizah.[88]

The amulets found clearly derive from various sources.[89] The Aramaic in these amulets can't be associated with a particular type of Aramaic, like *The Sword* can. They have qualities of magic from both Babylonia and the Land of Israel as well as midrashic and Talmudic magic, but they are most like the magical tradition of the Land of Israel,[90] which is exactly where *The Sword* comes from.

These amulets had various purposes—healing, love spells, to harm or get rid of an enemy, gaining favor with others, social acceptance, popularity, and success in business.[91]

These amulets use the *be-tem* formula ("in the name of God" followed by a divine name);[92] *The Sword* uses this formula only once. This is then followed by the same sort of stand-ins for the Tetragrammaton (YH, YY, H)[93] as are found in the Sword.

The amulets proceed with an adjuration and command for certain tasks to be done—this is very similar to the construction of the spells in *The Sword*—but these amulets are more extensive than the spells in *The Sword*. For instance, usually the client's name is given and the benefits of the amulet are listed—the longer the list, the better[94]—which resembles some of the first spells in *The Sword*. Biblical verses are used to back up the amulet (in *The Sword*, this information is not in the spells section but in what comes before), and the amulet ends with "Amen" or "Selah,"[95] which occurs rarely in *The Sword*.

Just as in *The Sword*, these amulets don't try to compel God—which does occur in Greek spells[96] and is one of the distinctions between Greek and Jewish magical texts. On the contrary, God's power is used to compel the angels in both amulets and *The Sword*. The magician holds the amulet and speaks it as an incantation,[97] just as the divine names are spoken in *The Sword*'s spells.

Jewish magic is highly involved with writing, and magical products of the time include writing of letters of the divine name and verses from the Hebrew Bible; these might be written in Hebrew or Aramaic, for the most part. They could be written on parchment or metal—metal amulets go back to the sixth and fifth centuries BCE—but they could also be written on leaves, glass, eggs, bone, papyrus, cloth, or leather.[98] Various other items could be used as non-written amulets, such as roots, knots, bells, grasshopper eggs, fox teeth, nails from a crucifixion, or a knot in the corner of a child's garment filled with salt, seeds, and shells meant for protection. These are all mentioned in rabbinic works of the early first millennium like the Tosefta* and the Mishnah.† [99]

---

* Text written in Jewish Babylonian Aramaic that compiles oral commentaries and supplements the Mishnah, written around late 100s CE.
† The Mishnah is the main compilation of oral commentaries and was written in Amoraic Hebrew in 189 CE.

The prevalence of knots in Jewish magic of this time period connects up to the word for amulet, which is *qame'a*. This is based on the root *qm'*, which means "to tie."[100] This root probably refers to how amulets were worn, often tied up in a pouch to be carried or worn around the neck or literally tied to one's arm, similar to *tefillin*.*

Materia Magica *of* The Sword's *Spells*

The *materia magica* of the spells in *The Sword of Moses* is different from that of *Sefer ha-Razim*, which is much more connected to Greek magic and the Hellenized world. In that book, the materials needed to work the spells would be familiar to an educated urban elite in any Hellenized culture. In contrast, the *materia magica* of *The Sword of Moses* consists of much simpler and more rustic items: vegetable oil, palm fibers, pottery sherds, and water, for instance. Only a couple of spells involve gold or silver lamellae, and no spells call for rings or carved gems, which do appear in *Sefer ha-Razim*.[101] Also, archaeologists have actually found brass lamellae with words from *The Sword of Moses* to silence or subdue opponents. These would be buried at doorways so that the target would walk over them.[102] So we can figure that *The Sword* was not meant to be used by sophisticated

---

* *Tefillin* are small leather boxes containing parchment pieces upon which are written specific verses from the Hebrew Bible. They have long straps. One is wound around the arm and on the hand forms the letter *shin*; the other is tied to the head. The straps on the head tefillin are tied in a knot representing a *daled*. Those of the arm tefillin are tied in a knot representing a *yod*. On the box for the head tefillin is a *shin*. Together these spell *Shaddai*, one of the names of the Divine, which has often been considered to be from the word for "breast" and thus an indicator that it designates a feminine aspect of God. This name is also present on the mezuzah, another kind of amulet for protecting one's home. Tefillin have been worn for at least 2,000 years and are still worn today during the morning service.

people in big cities but by more ordinary folk in towns. And we can see that some copies of it were actually personalized. For instance, five pages of *The Sword* were found in the Cairo Genizah, and those date from the eleventh to the twelfth century. In this version, instead of NN written in an adjuration where the client's name should be inserted, the copy has a real person's name, Mariot son of Nathan.[103]

Ethics of Spellwork in **The Sword.**

Another point to consider is that Jewish magical texts of late antiquity don't usually address whether it's right or wrong to use magic or whether morality forbids certain types of work.[104] Condemnation of any particular type of Jewish magic comes from outside the stream of Jewish magic. No late antique Jewish magician sits around ruminating over a Three-Fold Law or a slingshot effect. Some condemnation does come from the Rabbinic stream—even though rabbis also practiced magic, especially in order to accrue credibility, power, and control[105]—but often it was condemned as a foreign influence—as by Maimonides,[106] who nevertheless believed that "expert" written amulets—i.e., those that had brought results three times—were fine. The Rabbis were more likely to condemn conjuring or stage magic because it was trickery; they considered that otherwise magic, as long as it didn't assert impossible things like flying through the air, was real.[107] They even advised that if there were a drought, a magician should be hired.[108] Along those lines, any healing magic was fine, according to the Rabbis.[109] There does seem to be the implication that magical practices were condemned only when they were considered to be trickery; that's why Maimonides could say that amulets that actually worked were okay.

A Warning

The Sword of Moses ends with an instruction not to use the Sword inappropriately or the angels will attack and kill the magician. Again, we can see that these angels are not warm and fuzzy. To deal with them requires not only purification but courage.

WORKING TO WIELD
THE SWORD

The rite to gain the power to wield the Sword—the 1,800 divine names in *The Sword of Moses*—is relatively short at only three days, especially if we compare it to such rites as the Abramelin Operation, which may entail six months. But despite its brevity, it can still be a bit intimidating for the modern magician. This book's aim is to make it as simple and easy as possible while maintaining its authenticity and power.

You'll need to choose three days during which you do the rite. I originally thought that Friday, Saturday, and Sunday or a long holiday weekend provided a good option, and that might work well for some folks. But then I considered that, as a Jew, I didn't want to have to worry about breaking the Sabbath and violating its restrictions about using "fire" (which means electricity—I wouldn't be able to toast my bread) or cutting (I wouldn't even be able to cut slices). So I decided to choose three midweek days: Tuesday, Wednesday, and Thursday.

Remember that whichever days you choose, in Jewish tradition a "day" starts at sundown the day before. So for me, my three days would start at sundown on Monday and end at sundown on Thursday.

Since we're talking about days, another thing to consider is the length of the days. Remember that although you can drink water during the daytime, you should not eat until after sundown. If you are perhaps not an ace at fasting, consider doing this ritual in the winter, when days are short. The fasting time will be much longer in summer.

If you want to coordinate your fasting and purification with the moon phase, I would choose days so that your ritual ends on the full moon. This will give a little extra boost to the energy as the moon grows larger, the full moon being a typical time for the culmination of magical processes—although *The Sword* doesn't mention the moon at all.

If you want your ritual to coincide with astrological events, that is also an option but not mandated in any way or even mentioned. Just be sure to choose an astrological time that is positive, not, for instance, when Mars is ruling the heavens.

We are told that we should isolate ourselves, if possible, but we have seen that this isolation seems to be relative. For instance, we would not be cautioned to stay away from others or bake our own bread if we were in complete isolation. We wouldn't have any other choice. But *The Sword*'s author recognizes that different magic workers have different conditions to deal with. So we are advised to seclude ourselves.

What does this mean? It's typical in various works of Jewish mysticism of the time period of *The Sword*—both before and after its writing—that one who wants to ascend on high, for instance, or who wants to use the Tetragrammaton to attain the gift of prophecy, should do so from a separate room from which others can be excluded. *The Sword* contains nothing like a house in the middle of nowhere with a high spot from which one can observe the spirits called, as the Abramelin ritual does, but it is expected that we will be able to seclude ourselves.

The point of this is to keep away distraction, because remember: we are not calling spirits to appear before us. We are simply adjuring them to do what we wish in terms of magic. That's why we don't need a circle of protection or a triangle to keep spirits in. The angels we adjure remain in heaven. Our actions are intended merely to contact them.

But even that distant contact must be pure. I mentioned above that Jewish angels are nothing like the placid, gentle angels of the Victorian spiritualists. Instead, much like the spirits that Amazonian shamans deal with, Jewish angels are testy, dangerous critters. Purification allows us to interact with them safely. Being impure tempts them to act to destroy us, typically through fire, because Jewish angels tend to be Fire spirits: so, for instance, the Archangel Michael, a Fire spirit; the Ofanim—wheels of Fire; the Seraphim, wings of Fire; the angel at the gates of the Garden of Eden with its Fiery sword; and basically every level of angel in Hekhalot.

We start with ritual baths. Unlike in other magical practices, which allow for bathing in a basin or pouring water over one's head in the tub, Jewish ritual bathing requires living water. That means the water has to originate from a spring or be part of a river, a large lake, or the ocean. It can't be a pond. Can it be city water that comes out of your tap? Yes, if that's all you can do, but then it is really necessary to have a tub rather than use a shower, because ritual bathing in this practice involves dunking oneself completely under the water and, of course, nakedness. Some practices allow folks to wear very loose clothing for ritual cleansing, so you can for instance dunk yourself in the ocean in a loose bathing suit and this qualifies just fine as purification. But if you can, you should be naked. During my study for this book, I came across a ritual that demands the magic worker bathe twenty-four times per day. That means get into the water and dunk yourself twenty-four times. It doesn't mean take twenty-four baths. Even so, that would be a lot of dunking! With *The Sword*, we are asked to dunk only once, and we even don't have to do it each day for the three days.

For ritual bathing, first you clean yourself with soap and then after you have rinsed off, you dunk in living water. For this work, it is really important to avoid scent, even if it is a scent that we consider nice. We don't want to risk offending the angels, who we know are especially sensitive to scent. So use an unscented soap and fragrance-free shampoo. A simple, mild, pure soap is good. Dr. Bronner's has a fragrance-free version, for instance.

Next, we are advised to wear white clothing. Women might be able to get a white dress for this, but folks who prefer pants will find it a bit more difficult to get white ones, unless they are painter's pants. A really good alternative for magical work is Islamic clothing. It's inexpensive, you can easily find it online, they always have stuff that is pure white, they have big sizes, and there is a variety of styles. Thobes, which are just simple floor-length garments, are a good choice for men, and salwar kameez or kurtas/kurti for women. These are usually made of a mix of cotton and polyester. They are fairly well made for the price and very comfortable. Since we are not supposed to let ourselves get distracted from our work with this rite, being comfortable in our clothing is important.

But what if you aren't able to get white clothing? Choose blue—a blue shirt and jeans, for instance. Blue is closely associated with holiness in Judaism. It's the color of the Chariot, for instance. So this is a good fallback. Make sure it is some innocuous blue, if possible, like sky blue. And these should be comfortable and clean.

It's a good idea to wash three outfits and have them ready before you start the ritual. Just as with the soap for bathing, use a detergent that is fragrance-free and don't use any dryer sheets, as they are generally strongly scented.

Once you're clean and have your clean clothes on, don't use any scented items, like scented deodorant, cologne, or perfume.

What about the bread? The reason why we are told to eat only bread—and preferably of our own making—and to only drink water to break our fasts is because these things typically do not have any strong flavors or smells and they are not rich or "joyful," like wine or spicy foods. This doesn't mean you have to be somber, only that strong flavors are a distraction. Also, we are trying to network with angels, who don't eat. The Zohar says that angels consume only incense smoke, but this ritual does not call for incense and I would not use it, because, once again, it is a distraction.

For the bread, if you have a bread-maker or have made bread by hand before, and you don't have a problem digesting wheat, you won't have a problem. But what if you *do* have a problem with wheat? This was an issue for me, so I chose to make a quick bread combining chickpea and almond flour. Another good choice would be corn bread. You can bake enough for three days and then put the loaves in the freezer. Cut yourself off some slices at fast breaking and toast them in the toaster or a countertop oven to improve digestibility. Sprinkle with a tasty amount of salt before eating.

Eating bread is not supposed to be about punishing our body. In Judaism, the body is revered, considered a perfect work of the Divine. So we honor it, and not just in terms of refraining from doing things that will harm it, but we treasure and enjoy all the good things of the body: good eating, good sex, good sleeping, good exercise, etc. So it is good to enjoy our bread when we break our fast each evening.

Relative to refraining from harming the body, I thought of people who have diabetes and can't pile on a ton of carbs at any time, but especially not at night. That makes the directive to eat nothing but bread and water problematic. What you can do about this is put butter on your bread. There is nothing that says we cannot. It does not have a particular scent, and fat really helps to slow down the absorption of carbs, which if done too fast can make a diabetic person pretty sick. In my opinion, it is not an issue even for people who are not diabetic to do this, if it will make the fast easier to endure. After all, it is not the fast itself you are breaking if you put butter on your bread. And again, the point is not to make yourself miserable. It is to be ritually pure.

What about those of us who are hooked on caffeine? We are kind of out of luck on that score, since coffee does indeed have a smell, and a pretty strong one. If you get a bad headache during the day from not having your coffee fix, try some weak black tea with your fast-breaking. It will have little scent and is not that far from water, but it might be enough to cut the caffeine-withdrawal headache.

THE PRAYERS TO BE SAID

The prayer that we are asked to say three times a day in this ritual is called the Amidah, or Standing Prayer.

Can Non-Jews Do This Ritual, Including Saying the Amidah?

The short answer is *yes!* When we read the book *The Sword of Moses*, it is implied that the magic workers who would make use of its ritual

THE MAGIC OF THE SWORD OF MOSES

would be Jewish, and perhaps living in the northern area of the Land of Israel in the third quarter of the first millennium. We get that sense partly because of the use of Jewish Babylonian Aramaic and Hebrew, but also because the Amidah is a crucial part of the purification ritual. But does that mean that non-Jews didn't or can't use it? They can. In Isaiah 56:7, we read, "כי ביתי בית תפלה יקרא לכל העמים." "My house shall be a house of prayer to all nations." That means not only Jews can say prayers like the Amidah. Anyone can.

Saying the Amidah

If you have a prayer shawl, put it on and cover your head before saying the Amidah in the morning. (It's not worn for the afternoon or evening prayers, because we are told we should be able to "see" the ritual fringes.) Face east and put your feet together. The idea is that you take the same position you would before royalty. (Jews do not kneel.) Lots of people cover their head with their prayer shawl when saying the Amidah; it can help with concentrating, and I recommend it for saying the divine names also. Since we are advised to wear white clothes, a white prayer shawl is nice to use. You can easily find all sorts of prayer shawls online. Wool is traditional, but people also choose silk or rayon. Some prayer shawls are quite ornate and have a lot of patterns; many are decorated only with stripes—and width and arrangement of black stripes can inform others of the particular sect one belongs to, where your ancestors came from in Eastern Europe, whether one is a Zionist or not (blue stripes), or even if you practice Kabbalah (stripe colors are coordinated with the colors of the sefirot). Prayer shawls can especially honor the *Imahot* (the Mothers of the Hebrew Bible) or just be something shiny and glitzy. They can be small enough to be worn like a scarf or big enough for a couple to get married under. Really large ones can be kind of a pain to wear, and shiny ones are definitely a pain, slipping and sliding and making noise every time you move. The only vital thing about a prayer shawl, its main purpose, is the special knots at each corner. These have meaning outside of the commandment to wear them—how many knots and what kind can indicate whether you are from the Middle East or Western Europe, etc., and some even contain a blue thread, which might be colored with indigo, regular dye, or Tyrian purple (very expensive). I usually wear a black striped prayer shawl of wool with traditional generic knots in the corners, but I have a white one for holidays and for magic.

Nowadays, people who wear a prayer shawl usually bring the ends (where the fringes are) together and throw the ends up on each shoulder so it is easier to use a prayer book and nothing drags on the floor.

If you are not Jewish, you are not commanded to wear fringes on your clothes, so you don't need to wear a prayer shawl. But if you want to use one as a ritual garment, you can. It can be a helpful tool in that way, because it develops a sense of a border between the sacred and the mundane. In a way, it is like the magician's or witch's circle.

Also, you can go beyond simply wearing it across your shoulders and bring it up to cover your head, and, in this case, let the ends hang down to emphasize the feeling of being surrounded. Many people will actually bring it up so far that the front falls partly over their face, leaving enough space to read the prayer book. This helps to prevent distraction when praying, and I have to say that the first time I did this myself, I thought of a book I'd read about Muslim women who veil voluntarily. One woman said that in her veil she felt like she had her own personal mosque, a personal sacred space that she could have with her anywhere, even in public. I could totally understand that in my heart when I created my own personal sacred place by pulling my prayer shawl over my head in a synagogue, and I do it when I pray alone. I have even seen this practice concretized in old prayer shawls from Eastern Europe, which would sometimes have a section with a fancy border around it almost in the middle of the tallit. That area would rest as a crown upon the person's head when performing this withdrawal for prayer. I think that's a nice custom.

Since you are going to be pronouncing divine names, you should cover your head. I know that Christians take the opposite approach—uncover when praying or to show respect. But Jews and Muslims both cover their heads out of respect for holiness. This is not any kind of commandment but just a custom. It doesn't require any particular sort of headgear. You don't need to wear a skullcap. I have seen religious people wear a baseball cap, a bucket cap with fishhooks on it, a very expensive velvet fur homburg, a lace doily, and so on. It isn't something you have to do, and it is not mentioned in *The Sword*—not least of all because whether one should cover one's head or not has changed repeatedly in Jewish history. But it does form yet another boundary between the mundane and the sacred or magical, and to my mind, that is another way of helping to empower a ritual.

No one should be allowed to interrupt you when you are saying the Amidah or the adjurations. If someone asks you a question, don't answer. Some people will put their hand out indicating "stop" if someone speaks to them when they are saying the Amidah.

If you don't feel well or are tired, it is okay to sit instead of standing. What I have done is sit for the various adjurations before and during and after the Amidah, and stand for the Amidah unless I am dog-tired.

Before you start saying the Amidah, take three steps back, which represents withdrawing from mundane concerns, and then three steps forward to approach the Divine. At the end of the Amidah, take three steps back and then bow to the left, right, and forward and say the final part of the prayer, which is about the Divine granting us peace.

The Amidah is said three times a day by observant Jews. The first time is between sunrise and four hours later. The second time is 2.5 hours before sunset. The third time is between 1.5 hours before sunset to after sunset.

There are various versions of the Amidah. The most general division of types is one version to be said in public, one to be said in private, and one short version. I've included a private version and a short version. In Judaism, prayers can be changed as long as actual quotes from the Hebrew Bible are not being modified. (Such quotes can be removed or truncated, however.) For instance, several different Jewish denominations have removed references to the Temple's sacrificial cult, have changed the ways God is addressed so that it's gender neutral ("Holy One" instead of "King," for instance), have removed the reference to the resurrection of the dead or the return of the Jewish people to Jerusalem, and so forth. This is okay and allowed and does not decrease the validity or power of the prayer.

The main structure of the Amidah is in three chunks: praise of God, petitions, and thanks.

I created a version of the Amidah from Open Siddur, which is free culture/open copyright, meaning that anyone can use the material in any way for any purpose and can modify it.[1]

The Weekday Private Amidah

1. Ancestors

> I bless You, Holy One,
> God of Abraham and Sarah,
> God of Isaac and Rebekah,
> God of Jacob and Rachel and Leah.
> My life force and that of those who came before me.
> Life force of my mythic ancestors,
> Each of them wrestling with You in their own way.
> When I remember them, my own life is put in perspective:
> one strand in the weave of Your people.
> The force of life that came through my ancestors and
> became me
> is cosmic greatness, goodness, and loving-kindness.
> When I am aware that this force lives on through me
> I help redeem my generation and all those to come
> for the sake of Your love.
> You are my helper, my lover, my protector.
> I bless You, Holy One, whose love holds me in the arms of
> my ancestors.

2. Gevurot/Powers

> You are a beautiful and fierce lover-warrior, God.
> Your love wrests life from death.
> In the cycles of rain on the soil,
> And the cycles of growth in my soul
> You lift those who have fallen
> You heal those who are ailing
> You release those who are bound.

You keep firm faith with those who sleep in the dust.
Your presence slips into my heart even when I sleep
or want to be sleeping.
Who is like You, Master of Strength? Who compares to You?
You are life and You are death and You are the gardener who
    tends to both.
I affirm my trust in Your power to wrest life from death.
I bless You, Holy One, Who brings forth life from death.

3. Kedushat HaShem / Hallowing the Divine Name

You are holy and Your name is holy.
You are the balance between loving-kindness and justice.
I affirm Your ability to help me find that balance
as I am made in Your image.
I bless You, Holy One, Holy of Holies.

4. Binah/Understanding

Help me to reflect upon my actions
Help me to be aware of my thoughts
Help me to understand my emotions
that I may ever grow in balance, integrity, and compassion.
I bless You, Holy One, Who graciously grants me awareness.

5. Teshuvah/Return

Return me to You, Holy One!
Bring me close to You through service.
Circle me back to my whole heart
Which knows I belong to You.
I bless You, Holy One; those who return to You bring You joy.

6. Selikhah/Forgiveness

Forgive me, God
and help me forgive myself.
I am so imperfect and I judge myself so harshly.
Help me remember that perfection is Yours alone
and my job is to show up with courage and compassion
to my own messy human life.
I bless You, Holy One, Who forgives so much.

7. Ge'ulah/Redemption

See my struggles and help me with my troubles!
Bring me out of my stuck places so I can better be awake to
my life.
Redeem me quickly and with ease from the pain of shame.
I bless You, Holy One, Who redeems.

8. Refu'ah/Healing

Heal me, Nurturing One, and let me feel healed.
Save me, Holy One, and let me know I am safe.
Healed in body, mind, spirit,
Saved from the blight of my own fears. Heal me from perfec-
tionism and lust for results.
Save me from believing my own inner critics
and soothe my grief.
Send healing love to all those I hold in my heart today: [say
names here].
I bless You, Holy One, healer of all.

9. Birkat Hashanim/Blessing for Abundance

Bless me on Your good land, Abundant One.

Bless me with the courage and compassion to accept the bounty of Your Earth.

Bless me with the courage and compassion to accept the bounty of the years I have been given.

May I nourish my body.

May I eat and be satisfied.

May I greet each turning year with love and gratitude.

I bless You, All Bountiful One, Who nourishes my years.

10. Kibutz Galuyot/Gather the Exiles

I call out to You, Redeemer!

Let me witness the miracle when all the exiles return home to Your love.

Gather them in from the edges of the world and from beyond our sight

That all might be seen and heard and loved before You.

I bless You, Holy One, Who gathers in the exiles.

11. Din/Judgment

Loosen judgment's hold from my heart, Holy One.

Get me out of the judge's seat

Where I am exhausted and scared,

Where I dole out harsh rulings on myself and others.

Help me remember that You are the only judge, and You are compassionate.

I bless You, Wise One, Who loves compassion.

12. Birkat Haminim/Overcome Divisions

Let all those who act unjustly be defeated.
Let the evil of injustice disappear.
I bless You, Just One, Who uproots and transforms.

13. Tzadikim/The Righteous

Bless those who stand with courage
And protect those who choose the harder path to righteousness,
    Holy One.
Bless their small and great triumphs, Dear One,
And reward all who take shelter in You.
Let us never be ashamed that we trust in You.
Blessed are You, Trusted One, Who guides and supports the
    righteous.

14. Binyan Yerushalayim/Rebuilding Jerusalem

Holy One, may I feel You return to the places
that are wracked with conflict yet full of beauty.
May You dwell there again, as You said You would.
May I live gracefully in the paradox of longing for You
yet knowing You are with me all the time in total wholeness.
Draw out my holiest self, Blessed One, to serve You,
To be a messenger of the even better world that is coming.
I bless You, Holy One, Who builds wholeness.

15. Yeshu'ah/Salvation

Give me the strength to hope for my own transformation,
    Holy One.
Give me the discipline to envision my goals and

To take the steps necessary to achieve them.
I hope for the coming of your help.
I bless You, Holy One, saving grace of change.

16. *Kabbalat Tefillah/Accepting Prayer*

Hear my words, Holy One.
Help me build empathy, courage, and connection
that is stronger than my fears
Just as You hearken to our prayers with compassion
and do not turn us away with nothing.
Be gracious to me, and open my heart to hear my own longing
for gentleness, grace, and ease.
I bless You, Compassionate One, Who listens.

17. *Avodah/Worship*

May my struggles to grow be received as holy service.
May my breath, my softening, my moments of courage be
    received as sacrifices on the altar
And may they give You pleasure.
This is my devotional practice:
I offer my changing self to You, Faithful One,
Ever growing in love and trust
ever leaning in toward the belief that I am totally worthy just
    as I am.
I bless You, Holy One, Who receives my offerings with love.

18. *Hoda'ah/Thanks*

I humbly bow in thanks before You, Life of my life
for all the blessings I am aware of

and all the blessings I do not even think about.
I thank You especially right now for . . . [say what you are
especially grateful for right now]
I know that practicing gratitude fosters joy
and helps me build strength to endure hard times.
So I join my voice to all of life when I say
that I am grateful in every moment, every evening, morning,
and afternoon.
I bless You, Merciful One, receiver of my gratitude.
[take three steps back and bow to left, right, center]

19. Birkat Hashalom/Blessing for Peace

Help me feel the wholeness of my own heart, Dear One.
Amidst all my brokenness, let me feel how whole I am.
Help my loved ones feel their own wholeness too.
Lead me on a path of peace, to make peace with myself and
with others,
To find rest and integrity even as I struggle to grow.
I bless You, Eternal One, Who makes me whole.
May it be Your will to bless and protect me.
May it be Your will to shine Your light upon me.
May it be Your will to give me peace.
May the words of my mouth and the meditations of my heart
be received fully and with love.[2]

There is a short version of the Amidah that traditionally people
have used when they are very pressed for time or when traveling. I
think it is fine to use it when doing *The Sword* on account of the
length of the adjurations that come before and after the Amidah and

that are inserted into it. The short form keeps the beginning blessings (sections 1–3) and the concluding thanks (sections 17–19). In
this case, the adjurations meant to come after section 16 of the Amidah would just be said right after sections 1–3. This makes perfect
sense historically, since even now the Amidah is regularly modified
by removing the petitions of the middle section and replacing them
with a prayer about a holiday or other important issue at the time.

Adjurations

This is the prayer for protection from the fiery wrath of the angels
that you should say **before** the Amidah:

> Blessed is AhYoZaWaAh AhYoZaWaNuSa who went with
> Moses, and may that one walk along with me, whose name
> is AhHoWaTsaWaTsaYoHeh RehPehAhWaZaTaYoHeh
> RehPehWaAhTahZahYoHeh ZaHehWaGiYoHehYoHeh
> HehQoTsaTsaYoHeh EiNuTahWaTah-YoHehWaHeh GiDaWa-
> DaYoHehWaHeh WaYoNuYoEiTehTehWahQoTaZaYoHeh
> PehTsaPehYo PehYo AhZaYoHeh TehHehRehWaGiSaGiYoHeh
> ShiDaYoHeh QoTaTsaYoHeh RehHehWaMehYoh HehWaHeh
> TahGiPehMehTsaYoHeh AhHehYohWaPehSaQoTaYoHeh
> TaYoShiMehTsaYoHehYoHeh MehTsaHehWaGiTaHehYoHeh
> AhBehHehYoTaYoZaHeh QoPehHehWaHehYo RehPehTeh-
> GiWaTa RehPehRehPehTehReh YoMehRehTehRehYoHeh
> QoBehRehSaYoHeh NuKaDa QoTaSaNuYoHeh Meh-
> RehPehAhYoRehYoHeh GiNuTehSa- RehDa HehWaHeh
> DaYoDaAhRehRehAhHeh QoDaYoDaHehHeh QoGiYoTsa-
> HehHeh WaDaYoNuAhWaTsaYoHeh AhPehSaWaNuYoHeh
> AhYo PehYo LaYo MehAhSaSaWaNu PehRehQoWaMehYo-

Heh AhYo PehYo QoWaKhehZaYoHeh AhYoRehWaNuYoHeh
Ah-YoPehRehWaNuSaYoHeh AhPehSaYoWaAhHeh AhHeh-
YoHeh AhHeh DahYo, send me AhKhehRehYoAhWaSaSa-
HehWa YoHehWa QoTaSaHehHehYoHeh, who moves the
cherubim, may they aid me. Blessed is QoWaSaYoMeh for
ruling the sword.

This is the stream of adjurations to be said in the middle of the
Amidah right after blessing 16, which regards the Divine accepting
our prayer, or if using the short form of the Amidah, right after sections 1–3:

I conjure you, the four princes known as ShiQoDaKheh-
WaZaYo, MehRehGiYoYoAhLa, TehRehWahTehRehWaSaYo,
and HehDaRehWaYoZaLaWa, who serve HehDaYoRehYoReh-
WaNu YoHehWaHeh HehRehYoRehYoRehWaNu HehWa-
HehYo HehDaYoHeh.

DaYoHehYoRehWaNu HehWaHeh, before I even actually con-
jure you and before I supplicate you with my prayers, carry out
every request of mine through this sword just like you served
Moses. I entreat you through the powerful, wondrous, great
name HehWa HehYoHeh HehWaHeh SaPehReh HehWa-
Heh HehYoHeh YoHehWaHeh WaHeh YoHeh WaHehWa
YoWaHehHeh AhHehWaSaHehHeh YoHehHeh QoQoSa
HehWaHeh. That one should conjure the five princes above
them and say: I conjure you, MehHehYoHehWaGiTsaYoYo
PehKhehDaWaTaTaGiMeh AhSaQoRehYoHehWa ShiYoTahYo-
NuYoKhehWaMeh QoTaGiNuYoPehYoYo HehDaWaDaYo

WaHehWaHeh YoDa GiBehRehYoAhLa YoHeh HehWa
HehDaYoRehYoRehWaNu to do what I ask before I even
ask it and that you bind yourselves to me and that you further
bind to me these four princes and all the hosts of those
princes over whom you rule to carry out my desires through
the use of the sword and by this most loved name: AhHehYo
HehWaHeh YoHeh WaHeh AhYo AhWa HehHehYo HehWa-
HehYo ShiHehWaSaHehHeh YoWaHeh HehWa HehWaWa
YoHeh YoHehHeh YoWaHeh HehYoYo. And that one should
conjure the three princes above them and say: I conjure you,
AhSaQoWaHehHehYo ShiTehRehYoSa HehWaYoHah SaHeh-
WaTaGiYoAhYoHeh, the ones whom ZaRehHehWaDaReh-
YoNu, that is HehDaYoRehYoRehNu, loves, bind to me those
under your authority, MehHehYoHehWaGiTsaYoYo PehKheh-
DaWaTaTaGiMeh AhSaQoRehYoHehWa ShiYoTaYoNuYo-
KhehWaMeh QoTaGiNuYoPehYoYo ShiQoDa KhehWaZaYo
MehRehGiYoYoAhLa HehDaRehWaYoZaLaWa. Have them
carry out my wishes through the power of this name: Heh-
Heh HehWaHeh HehWaYo ShiQoTsaDa HehShiHeh HehYo
AhWa HehWa HehHeh YoHehHeh PehTaTehGiHehWa
HehHeh YoHeh YoHehWa HehWa Heh-YoYo WaHehYo
YoHehNuYoHeh WaNuHehHehYoHeh MehTaGiMehHeh-
WaHeh Heh-YoQoHehHeh WaHehYo HehAh TsaRehMeh-
QoWaQoTahTsa YoHeh HehYoHeh WaHehYo HehHeh
TahSa HehWaWa HehYoHeh YoHehWa HehYo HehYoHeh
WaYoHeh TaYoHeh ZaYoHeh TaHehWaHehYo. That one
should command the prince who rules over them all, saying:
I conjure you, AhHehYoWaPehSaQoTaYoHeh, who is great
and mighty, the commander of all the hosts of heaven, that

you yourself, and not your messengers, be bound to me, and that you further bind for me your princes so that they carry out my wishes through the power of this sword, using the singular name: YoHehWaWaHeh AhHehHeh HehWaHeh Heh-HehYo HehHeh AhYoHeh HehYoHeh HehWa HehWaHeh YoHehWaHehYo HehWa HehYo WaHehYoHeh WaHehHeh AhHehWaHehYo HehHehYo AhHeh WaHehWaHehYo YoHeh WaHeh AhHeh WaHeh AhHeh YoWa HehYo HehWa HehYo HehYoHeh HehHeh WaHeh YoHehWa HehWaYoHehWaYo HehHehWaHeh YoHehWa YoHehWa, for like you, I, the seed of Abraham, who was beloved, am loved, and the Holy One is called beloved. Praise be to You, YoHehWaHeh, Ruler of secrets and of mysteries, who heeds our prayers.

This is the prayer and set of adjurations to be said after you say the Amidah:

You are blessed, QoWahSaYoMeh, our God, Ruler of the world, the Holy One who every morning throws open the eastern gates and breaks open the windows of the east to light the entire world. The Divine One blesses those who live on Earth with merciful abundance, with divine mysteries and holy secrets. That One taught the people Israel what had been unrevealed and hidden and showed them a sword that can mold the world. QoWahSaYoMeh told them: When you are ready to wield this sword, which fulfills all wants, uncovers all mysteries, tells all secrets, and enacts marvels, wonders, and miracles, say these words to me, recite them to me, and conjure them to me. Then I will accept them right away and accommodate you and put you in charge of this sword so that it will do whatever you

ask it. Those princes named will agree to help you. My holy
spirits will accommodate you. They will carry out your wishes
instantly, reveal to you my mysteries and all that which I con-
ceal. They will tell you how to say my words and will show you
my miracles. And they will say with you and help you like an
apprentice to a master. And your eyes will see and your heart
will envision and understand everything that is now occulted,
and you will grow in reputation and power:

I call you, SaWaQoYoMeh, Ruler of the universe.
You're called YoHehWaGiHeh HehWa AhLa YoHeh—Ruler of
    the Universe.
You're called PehAhZaWaGiHeh WaHeh WaWa AhLa YoHeh
    —All-merciful Ruler
You're called ZaHehWaTah GiYoHehHeh AhLa YoHeh—Ruler
    of graciousness
You're called TsaHehBehRehWaHehWa HehWaHeh AhLa
    YoHeh—Living Ruler
You're called SaPehTsaHehWaTaHehWa AhLa YoHeh—Hum-
    ble Ruler
You're called QoGiYoWaHehYo HehWa HehYo AhLa
    YoHeh—Righteous Ruler
You're called ShiHehRehWa SaGiHehWaRehYo AhLa
    YoHeh—Ruler on high
You're called SaPehQoSa HehPehYoHehWaHehHeh AhLa
    YoHeh—Ruler without flaw
You're called QoTaTaHehWa GiTaHehYo AhLa YoHeh—Ruler
    without falsity
You're called PehTaRehYoSa HehZaPehYoHehWa AhLa
    YoHeh—Mighty Ruler

THE MAGIC OF THE SWORD OF MOSES

You're called RehEiPehQo TsaYoWaYoHehYoHeh AhLa
    YoHeh—Chosen Ruler
You're called KhaWaSaHeh YoHehWaHehYo AhLa YoHeh—
    Proud Ruler
You're called WaHehWa HehWa HehYo HehYo AhHehYoHeh
    WaHeh YoHeh YoHeh WaHeh YoHeh WaHeh YoWa HehYo
    HehYoWa YoHeh
You hear my prayer because you hear everyone's prayers. Oblige
    the ones who serve you—the princes named in the Sword—
    to do what I say, because you rule them, and you will have
    them carry out all my desires since your hands hold every-
    thing, as it is written: "You open your hand and fulfill the
    desires of every living being" (Ps. 145:16).

I charge you, AhZaLaYoAhLa, whom they call HehWaDaYo
    ZaHehYo HehWa HehWaHeh,
AhRehAhLa, whom they call SaQoRehYoSaYoHehYoHeh,
TehEiNuYoAhLa, whom they call AhTaRehTsa AhHehYoHeh
    YoHeh,
TehPehAhLa, whom they call GiWaPehQoYo HehWaHeh
    AhHehYoHeh,
and the most powerful of all: HehLaYoKaYoHeh, who is
    YoWaPehYoAhLa,
MehYoTehTehRehWaNu, whom they call GiHehWaDaPehTeh-
    HehWa HehHeh YoHehHeh HehDaReh MehRehWaMeh,
    MehRehShiWaTa MehLaKaYo YoDaYoAhLa, whom they
    call SaGiHehWaHeh HehYoHeh,
RehEiShiYoAhLa, whom they call MehHehWaPehTaQoYoHeh-
    Heh YoYo,

KhehNuYoAhLa, whom they call RehHehWa PehGiTaYoHeh,

HehNuYoAhLa, whom they call PehHehWaTsaPehNuYoGiYo-
Heh,

EiShiRehAhLa, whom they call TaHehMehWaTaYoHehYoHeh-
YoHeh,

WaYoShiDaYoAhLa, whom they call QoNuYoTaYo PehTsahYo-
Heh,

EiShiHehAhLa, whom they call YoHehWaTa NuTehHehYo
HehYoHeh,

EiMehWaDaYoAhLa, whom they call RehWaPehNuYoGiYo-
Heh WaSaSaYoHeh,

WaAhTsahRehAhLa, whom they call ShiHehGiNuWaTaGiYo-
HehHeh,

I charge all of you to serve me and to make the sword subject
to me in order that I can utilize it any way I want and be
protected in the secret place of the Mighty One above[3] in
heaven.

I charge you by this noble, powerful, and awe-inspiring name,
which is made of the twenty-four letters that rest upon
the diadem of the Holy One: HehWa HehYo HehHehYo
HehWa HehHeh AhHeh WaHeh YoHeh YoHeh Heh-
WaYo HehWa HehYo HehWa HehWaHeh YoHehWa YoAh
HehWa HehWa YoHeh YoHehWa HehYo HehWa YoAh
YoHeh WaHeh HehWa YoAh HehWa HehWaYo HehYoWa
HehWa YoHeh WaHeh YoHeh HehWa HehWaHeh YoHeh-
Yo HehWa YoHeh AhHehYoHeh MehHehWaHeh, render
unto me by the means of this sword revelation of the secrets
and hidden knowledge of the worlds above and below. Carry
out my desires, heed my commands, and fulfill my wishes;

obey my words and accede to my requests. By saying aloud the following name as an adjuration, a holy name that is honorable and dependable, the highest divine name that binds and ties all of the hosts of heaven:

HehHeh HehHeh HehWaHeh HehHehYoYo YoWaHehHeh AhHeh WaHeh NuYoHeh HehWaHeh PehHeh WaHehWa HehYoHeh TsahHehWa AhHeh WaHeh HehYoHeh Heh-Heh WaHeh YoHeh WaHeh YoHeh SaYoHeh WaHeh YoHeh WaYoHeh, may that name be blessed, I charge to hurry to carry out my requests and not to hurt me, frighten me, or terrorize me. Your ruler, whom you honor and whose might terrifies you, reveres this name, and by this name, which they call PehRehZaMehWaTaGiYoHeh SaRehKhehWaQoTaYoHeh HehYoGiNu-YoTaYoHeh TehRehSaNuYoHehYoHeh QoReh-ZaMehTaHehWa TsaGiYoHeh YoHeh WaHeh HehYoHeh HehWa HehYo HehAh HehWaHeh HehWaHeh AhHehHeh HehHehYo AhHeh WaHeh HehWaHeh HehYoHeh AhHeh WaHeh YoHeh YoHehHeh YoHehWa YoHehYo AhWa Heh-Heh AhHeh HehHeh HehAh HehYoHeh AhHeh ZaQoRehYo-DaRehYoHeh do what I have asked you to and be a servant to me as your master, because I adjure you not by the name of your princely overseer but by the Holy One who rules above all and by that Holy One's name you and all the spirits of heaven are bound, connected, tied, and caught. I will turn you over to that Aweful One, to the Divine One, blessed be the Holy One's inexpressible name, if you do not come to me quickly and obey me speedily, the fury and rage and fiery, burning energy of the Divine One. All of the Holy One's universe worships that inexpressible name, one of the letters of which is called ZaRehWaGiDaQoNuTehAh QoTsahWaPehTsahKhehTaYo-Heh AhHehWaHeh SaQoTaYo GiYoHeh GiYoGiYoMeh HehYoGiYoHeh HehWa YoHeh HehNuYoHeh HehWaHeh QoLaTsahGi. If you don't hurry to come to me and serve me, That One will obliterate you and all who search for you will not find you. Defend me from my own recklessness and from doing myself any injury in the name of KhehZaQoAhYo AhHehYoHeh WaHeh YoHeh HehHeh YoHehHeh YoHeh WaHeh HehHeh YoHeh HehYoHeh AhHehYoWa YoHeh HehYoWa YoHehYo WaHehWaYo HehYo HehWaYo YoHeh QoQoHehWaHeh SaQoQoHehWaHeh, who watches over the people of Israel. You are blessed, SaWaQoYoMeh, you are the ruler of the world, wise in mysteries and revealing secrets.

This is another series of divine names to recite after the Amidah:

This is the mighty and just name that was given over to human beings to use: YoHeh BehYoHeh AhTsah AhHeh BehAhHeh HehWaYo HehWa HehWa WaHeh YoAh HehWa ZaHeh WaHeh WaHeh AhHeh YoHeh YoHehWa HehHeh YoHehWa YoHehWa AhQoPeh HehYo HehHeh YoYoAhHeh HehHeh HehAhHeh HehWaAhHeh HehHehWaHeh HehYoYo HehWa HehWa HehYo divine almighty powerful. Selah.

The names of the heavenly spirits who serve human beings are: MehYohTehTehRehWahNu, SaGiDaDaTaTsaYoHeh and MehQoTehTehRehWaNu, SaNuGiWaTaYoQoTaAhLa, and NuGiYoQoTaGiAhLa, and YoGiWaAhTaQoTaYoAhLa, and AhNuTaGiQoSaAhLa, and AhNuTaWaSaSaTaYoAhLa,

and MehYoKaAhLa SaRehWaGi, and GiBehRehYoAhLa*
ShiQoTaKaNuYoHeh, and HehDaQoRehWaNuTaYoAhLa,
and AhNuHehSaGiAhLa, YoHehWaAhLa, TaYoZaRehTa,
NuSaYoAhLa, and SaYoGiSaTehHehAhLa, and AhNuPehYo,
QoQoPehYoAhLa, and NuHehReh, GiSaGiNuHehYoAhLa,
and YoKaNuYo, AhTaYoHehAhLa, and AhQoTaQoLaYo-
QoAhLa, YoNuHeh, GiYoTaNuYoAhLa YoHeh. Serve me,
[your first name], child of [your father or mother's first name],
and hear my prayer and what I want and bring it to the attention of YoHehWaHeh HehHeh SaHehHeh AhHehHeh Heh-
Heh WaHeh WaHeh, who is the blessed Holy One. I charge
you in that name and exact your vow as neatly as a bird settling
in its nest. Tell the Holy One about my merits and plead with
That One to forgive me my sins immediately. Do not wait
to do so, in the name of SaHeh HehHeh WaHeh WaYoHeh
YoHeh WaYoHeh WaHeh WaHeh WaYoHehHeh WaYoHeh
EiHeh HehHehWaYo EiHehWa YoEi HehYo HehYo HehWa
HehWa YoHehWa HehHeh HehWaHeh YoHeh WaHeh
blessed be the Holy One of Hosts. Selah. Let the servants of
the Divine One sweetly bless and worship That One, singing
"Holy holy holy is the Ruler of the universe; the whole world is
filled with the Divine One's glory" (cf. Is 3:3). Do not encum-
ber the power of the order given by HehWa HehYoHeh YoHeh
HehWa YoYo YoHehWa HehYo HehYo HehWaHeh HehYo
HehWa HehHeh HehHehYoHeh HehYo HehWaHeh HehYo-
Heh HehWaYoHeh YoHehWa HehHehWa HehHeh HehHeh-
WaYo YoHehWa AhHehWa HehHeh YoHeh AhHehHeh

---

* This is clearly the name Gabriel. In fact, all the names that end in YoAhLa are names of
the type we would recognize as ending with -iel.

AhYoHeh AhYo AhHeh AhYo AhHeh WaHeh YoHeh, who
lives forever. In the name of DaYoTehYoMehYoNu QoYoReh-
WaYoAhSa WaHehWa AhRehQoMeh GiNuLaYoAhWaSa
QoWaSaMehWaSa QoLaYoQoSa AhSaQoLaYoTehTaRehAh
AhYoLaYo AhLaYo MehWaPehYo SaPehRehAh SaTehGiDaAh-
GiSa TehLaAhSaYo QoTehMeh AhNuTa PehRehGiWa
PehYoGiHeh DaYoHehYo MehYoTaQoAhSa NuPehLaAh
TaTehAh DaWaNuYoTehAh TaTaMehNuAhSa TehWaPeh
DaWaGiZa MehTehYoGiAh MehHehWa WaHehWaTeh-
Reh ZaYoQoQoTaYoHehWa AhHehWaNuYo YoHehWa
YoHeh AhLa KhaYoNuQoYoHeh PehPehTehYo HehYoAhSa
SaPehTsaPehNuTehReh; and in the name of SaMehRehTa
SaMehSa PehTsaTsa AhDaWaNuWaKhaTa HehWaSaYoHeh
AhLaYoWaNu YoHeh HehWaAhYo AhWa HehYoHeh PehYo
PehYo AhYoTaYoHeh WaBehTsaRehSa MehTsaRehPehYoHeh
TaSaQoYoHehWa BehShiTaQoTsaReh the Lofty One, who
sees everything yet is not visible, who knows all secrets; and
in the name of TehYoRehQoTehTaYoHeh, who rules over the
heavens and whom they call YoHehWa YoHehWa WaHeh
YoHeh YoHeh AhHeh AhYoWa WaHeh Nu-YoHehWa HehYo-
Heh HehYo HehYo YoHehYo WaHehYo HehWaHeh YoHeh-
Wa HehYoHeh HehYoHeh WaHeh HehWaHeh HehHeh
WaYoHeh YoYoHeh WaHehYo HehYo YoHehWa
HehYo, whose name is glorified and honored, and which the
ruler of the universe says in various ways, such as: YoHeh-
Wa AhHeh YoHeh WaHehHehHeh YoHeh WaHeh YoHeh
YoHehWa HehHeh YoHeh HehWa HehWaWa HehYo
HehYo HehHeh HehYo HehWa HehWaAh HehWa HehYo-

Heh HehWaYoHeh YoHeh WaHeh YoHeh WaHeh YoHeh
YoHeh HehYo HehYo HehYo AhHehHeh AhHehYo HehWa
HehHeh YoHeh YoHehYo HehWa HehWaHeh YoHehWa
HehWa HehHeh YoYoHehWa HehHeh YoYoWa; I charge
you by these names, swift messenger: Don't delay or make me
tremble. Come and do all I ask, I [your first name], child of
[your mother or father's first name]; do what is necessary to
fulfill all my needs, in the name of YoHehWa HehHehYoWa
YoHehWa AhHehYoWa HehHehWa HehWa HehYoHeh Heh-
HehYo HehWaHeh YoHeh WaHeh HehHehYo YoHeh HehWa
HehYoWa HehYoHeh WaHehWaTehReh QoTaNuGiYoHeh
ZaWa QoWaSaSaYoHeh AhHehWaNuYoHeh AhLa HehYo
NuQoTaSaAhLa YoHeh HehWaHeh NuYoGiGiHehHeh Peh-
SaQoTaRehHeh HehYo HehWaHeh YoHeh ZaRehWaMeh-
TaHeh HehYoHeh WaBehReh ShiTehHeh HehYo HehHehYo-
Heh, the exalted, who sees everything and yet remains invisible;
AhHehWaHeh, all the heavenly spirits learned the meaning of
this name, and I charge you by the meaning of that name, as
it was told to Moses, son of Amram, from Holy One's mouth,
YoHehWaHeh WaHehAhHeh HehWaHeh YoHehWaHeh
HehYoHeh HehWa HehHehNuYoHehHeh YoHeh HehYo
HehYo HehWa HehHeh YoHehWaHeh SaHeh HehHeh
WaHehYoHeh WaHehHeh HehWaHeh YoHeh YoHeh YoHeh-
Yo LaNuHehHeh YoHeh YoHeh AhHeh TaBehYoNuWa AhYo-
Heh YoHehWaShi AhHehYoShiHeh WaAhGiReh-YoPeh-
Teh YoHehWa TsahBehAhWaTah YoHehWaHeh YoHehWa-
Heh TsahBehAhWaTa is That One's name. Blessed are You,
Holy One, Ruler of the powerful and knower of the occult.

Yes, it's a lot, but hang in there. As you practice using the Natural Vowels to say the divine names, you'll begin to hear these long strings of words as melody. Go with it. All Jewish prayers are sung, so there's no reason why Jewish magic should not be. It makes it easier to carry on with long sections of words, and it beautifies them. And beauty not only makes holy but also adds power to magic.

THE SPELLS

One of the most notable things about these spells is that there is no judgment as to whether it is right or wrong for the magic worker to carry them out. There is no warning, no caution, except with respect to our behavior toward the angels and the necessity of our purity when we try to interact with them. But whether it is all right to cast a spell to kill someone is not addressed. We see nothing about potential punishment or even danger in doing this. There is no karma, no threat of Hell, no slingshot effect, no threefold return of doing something bad—or good, for that matter. And of course we hear nothing about whether magically forcing a man or woman to come to us for sex is ethical. Binding seems to be just fine in *The Sword*. Instead, the book clearly expects us as magic workers to judge for ourselves whether we need to do any of the cursework described here.

I think one reason for this is that this is not a religion, even though angels are called upon and bound because of promises made to one of the patriarchs of a religion. It's not a philosophical work; it's a do-it-yourself book.

Another notable lack shows up around animal sacrifice. There is only one spell that involves its use, and that is a spell for casting nightmares that calls for slaughtering a rooster exactly as it would have been killed in order for it to be eaten. I didn't include that here, because there are other spells for casting dreams. But contrast this to

The Greek Magical Papyri, where we are told to crucify a hawk to a wheel and spin it around and beat it in order to make a woman have sex with us. This is a different world.

What strikes me most about this—setting aside the question of whether it is ethical to kill animals—is the assumption of *The Sword of Moses* that all a determined magician needs in order to kill someone are the divine names. Remember the story about Moses using the divine names to kill the Egyptian overseer who was beating a Hebrew? It's typical for the Rabbis, when describing magic done by past sages, much less patriarchs like Moses, to remark: "Well, we can't do that nowadays because they were great and we are small, they were holy and we are not," etc. But there is nothing like that in *The Sword of Moses*. We are, it is assumed, just as qualified to do killing magic as Moses was. In fact, it is *because* Moses did it and received the gifts of the angels that we can do it too. We don't need to be born with a caul, to be the seventh son of a seventh son, to have come up in a family tradition. Nothing. Just the names and the rather short ritual preparation that will enable us to use them. Compare this, for instance, to the Abramelin Operation, where the ritual preparation can be six months long. Now it's true: *The Sword of Moses* does not contain spells on the scale of destroying armies, like Abramelin does. But the spells are no small potatoes either. And really, when was the last time you needed to destroy an army?

Divine names are pretty heady stuff.

The other interesting point, although of less import with respect to how our magical practice might affect others, is what is *not* here. There are no wealth spells or spells for finding hidden treasure. I consider the reason for that is any magic worker of that time using these spells professionally would already be making a good living and not have any need for wealth spells or treasures. A magic worker would be respected in their community, and respect usually comes with reward in many human societies—and other animal societies too, for that matter.

It's also interesting that such spells would not be offered to clients. Clearly, clients were not coming to magicians to ask them to do a spell to get rich. There aren't even any gambling spells here.

Even though the protection of pregnancy and especially newborns came to be very popular in Jewish folk magic, we don't find such spells in *The Sword* either. There are not even charms for fertility.

We get a sense of the customers of the magic worker who wrote this book when we notice none of the revenge against a bad boss–type spells we might find in other practices. That implies that the clients of a magic worker using *The Sword* were not generally ordinary laborers. Instead, outside of the healing spells, it feels like the primary clients were tradespeople and merchants.

At the same time, *The Sword of Moses* does not read like many medieval or Renaissance grimoires written by European priests to be sold to nouveau riche merchants. It has often struck me, when looking at such grimoires, that the exotic ingredients called for in such works are there precisely in order to prevent the user from actually carrying out the magic. If the magic can never be proven to work or may not work because you can't find the materials to do the spell, no newly wealthy merchant who handed over a bucket of money to an unemployed priest will ever go back to them and demand their money be returned for item not working as advertised.

In contrast, most of the spells in *The Sword* don't call for any *materia magica*, and when materials are involved in the spells, they are what would have been common items at the time: leaves of ordinary plants, eggs, sticks, and so forth. The most expensive thing mentioned is a silver dish.

Other objects not mentioned are any kind of wand, a consecrated knife or an actual sword, an altar, a ritual cup, a particular type of robe, a blasting rod—in fact, there is a distinct lack of props in this path. Even the few talismans seem to be quite plain, composed of ordinary letters on a surface that is usually not even described. There is no magic ink—no description of ink at all in any way.

And most of all, there is no incense. No scent at all. I wonder if this is not because we are cautioned not to recreate the Temple incense, especially for any purpose other than honoring God. But it might also be because it is just deemed unnecessary. We already have everything we need to do the magic, whether it is getting rid of someone's headache or killing them, solely through the divine names.

I think this lack of props is due to the consideration of the extraordinary power of the names. We don't need an actual ritual sword with stuff engraved on it—nice as such things are—because we have the Sword composed of divine names.

A SELECTION OF SPELLS

The types of spells found generally in Jewish magic certainly occur in *The Sword of Moses*: harming, healing, love, and knowledge.[1] To those I would add protection and path-jumping. I also include here some miscellaneous spells just because they are interesting.

Most of the spells are quite specific about their action, but the first two spells described in *The Sword* are very broad in terms of what they will do for the magic worker. I am not sure why that is the case, but I have a sense that they both came from the same source, one that provided only these two very floppy spells. None of the rest of the spells are as all over the place as these two are. However, I do consider that perhaps the magician who compiled these spells put them first because they thought they were the most useful or were spells that were most often used.

General Spells

At the full moon, use this spell **to take and bind a couple together** so that they will have sex with each other and/or will not be unfaithful to each other. This spell is also useful **to destroy evil spirits**, *satans* (spirits that oppose humans), and blast demons.[*] It can also be utilized **to stop a boat from moving forward**. Someone who is **incarcerated can be freed** through the use of this spell. It is also generally helpful, the implication being that perhaps it comes first in the manuscript because it is the most general.

In each case, write the section of the Sword necessary to empower the spell on a red[†] plate:

The manuscript does not explain whether anything further is done with the plate. But one thing I have noticed about this work is that it assumes a certain amount of experience with magic—not

---

[*] A blast demon is a spirit responsible for causing harsh winds that destroy crops or, more metaphorically, that destroy belongings. The sense is that whatever is the target of this demon is blown away or dispersed uselessly.

[†] An interesting association with Mars. This implies the use of wormwood, a Martial herb.

תוכר תסכר אכן טטה מיטס
אגדו אכקא דיוקטאס לסוס
אנתן סדופיפלא ססא
או או
הופהאטא
היפורקסטא
מונכגדין: מנגנין נט נטלאס
דינקא דיסוקסא גהיא טאקם
קוסמו יה הידרסא:
הידדסטא
אנטא דימנא דאימנא הינ
טלאין טלאוס פאמוטום
אטופדמא

to an advanced state, but enough to be familiar with the territory
and not either panicked by demons or too timid to throw curses. I
think how and if the plate is further used depends on the nature of
the spell it energizes and on what the magician believes is appropriate. To bind a couple together, for instance, could involve writing
the divine names with honey and washing them off into some wine
that will be served to the target couple. If using it to stop a ship, the
magic worker might decide to put it in a net and throw it into the
sea, a net allowing it to be retrieved when it's wished to reverse the
spell. If repelling evil spirits, it might be a good idea to bury it at the
threshold of the client's house.

The second spell in the manuscript is just as wide-ranging as the first but covers different issues. This spell is useful for flattening mountains and crossing both sea and land safely—a process called **path-jumping**, about which there are several spells below. It is intended to protect you if you need **to descend into fire and return safely.** You can use it **to overthrow a ruler.** It can help you **create optical illusions.** Just as above, it can **halt a ship.** It can **stop someone from talking** or from spreading lies or information harmful to the user. It is an instrument **for speaking with the dead**, on the one hand, or **dispatching the living**, on the other. It empowers the adjurations of angels, who will descend and must obey your commands and teach you **all the universe's secrets**, and then can be utilized to dismiss them.

Here's the spell. The following should be written on a silver plate onto which a root of artemisia is placed.* The same section of the Sword that is used in spell 1 is used here; however, no moon phase is mentioned. Even so, a number of the tasks it covers have a Water/Moon feel to them, which makes sense of the silver plate:

---

* This could have been *Artemisia herba-alba*, aka white wormwood, which is often available in the United States as an essential oil replacement for wormwood (*Artemisia absinthium*), although it has, in my opinion, a sweeter smell than wormwood essential oil. I think it would be fine to use other members of this family, since they invariably have similar uses, regardless of the culture that makes use of them. They are often good for banishing, for instance. I would try mugwort for the more benevolent spells and wormwood for the aggressive spells or curses. Both are *Artemisia* species. Even better would be to grow the plant yourself, as artemisias tend to be very easy to grow and, if anything, if planted in the ground will pretty much take over your yard.

```
תוכר תסכר אכן טטה מיטס
אנדו אכקא דיוקטאס לסוס
אנתן סדופיפלא ססא
או או
הופהאטא
היפורקסטא
מונכנדין: מנגנין נט נטולאס
דיניקא דיסוקסא נהיא טאקם
קוסמו יה הידרסא:
הידדסטא
אנטא דימנא דאימנא הינן
טלאין טלאוס פאמוטום
אטופדמא
```

Healing Spells

The Sword of Moses contains a large number of healing spells that deal with very specific illnesses. Everything from earaches, deafness, and jaundice to stab wounds, gallstones, miscarriage, and even hemorrhoids are covered. Due to concerns about space, I chose a few I thought would be more generally helpful to someone who is more of a magician than a physician.

For instance, I suspect most magic workers more often deal with someone being attacked by a spirit than by gallstones. This spell is helpful when someone is **plagued by a spirit infesting their entire body**. In that case, write a talisman made up of the following and have them carry it with them or wear it. It doesn't matter what you write it on. You can even write these divine names on the individual's body; there is a tradition of writing divine names on the body for protection. These are the names:

הידדסטא
אנטא דימנא דאימנא הינן
טלאין טלאוס פאמוטום
אטופדמא

A similar spell addresses the situation of a **demon haunting a place or bothering a person or animal**. The spell advises that the magician write the following divine names as a talisman to banish it. You can write them on anything that can be carried or worn or put them on the person's skin or on a garment they will wear. If you are dealing with a place, write the names on something convenient, such as a piece of paper to be hung in the area, or even directly on the wall as graffiti. Writing it as graffiti might well help dispel evil spirits from abandoned places; such places often seem to become haunted by negative spirits:

While some spirits enjoy hanging around old warehouses, other probably more dangerous ones seem to delight in torturing people. This spell addresses a particular type of **evil spirit that gives eternal terror**, nightmares, loneliness, and dread and can cause the mental disintegration of a human being. This type of spirit doesn't necessarily have a name but is known from one of the incantation bowls[2] that were created for someone who clearly was being horribly tormented by such a spirit. Considering that the incantation bowls were found mostly in Iraq and *The Sword* was written in the Land of Israel, we've

הא בשמהת כולכון וכנוייכון

דרבריתון אתון בכל אתר

לית דכותכון אוחן ואבעו ואיתו

לית אססיה אסס ואססית

ואפרנסיה ירונקא

ירך ירץ יהץ יקץ

ויעביד לי כל צניוע

יוא בשם יאו

יהוהה יההיה

אוזרוס סומרטא

got a fairly well known, prevalent, and obviously very dangerous spirit. Perhaps the reason why it does not have a name is because it is one of those entities that is drawn by its name being spoken.

Against this spirit, *The Sword* advises creating a talisman featuring the following divine names:

יאו יהו אן ליהו פאדי ינא

אבכסס לוקיאס נססתיה

נכסתא נססתא יזאוס

יואוס יואו יזאו

יאו יאיי יאיי אדוני אדוני

As usual, no particular ink or support—whether paper, parchment, metal, or whatever—is prescribed, so choose what you feel would work best for the client. If a metal is selected, I would advise iron, since typically that metal banishes spirits. If using paper or parchment, consider making an ink from iron oxide pigment. You can usually find a nice deep red made of this substance from those who supply artists with pigments or from suppliers for cosmetic and soap manufacturers. Just dissolve some powdered gum arabic in a little warm water, mix in the pigment, and add about 15–20 percent alcohol as a preservative. Any pigment you'd like to use as an ink should be very finely powdered, and often it helps when putting it into suspension in water to first mix it with a little high-proof alcohol. Use with a dip pen or even a reed, which would be wonderfully fitting for these spells.

This next spell combines defending against a demonic attack by a palga spirit with the **healing of a migraine**. Palga spirits are mentioned in the Talmud in the volume called *Pesachim* 111b, which describes a man being afflicted with a migraine after peeing on a palm tree stump, which just so happens to be the kind of place where palga spirits like to hang out. Angered by the person's disrespect, the palga spirit takes revenge by giving the man a splitting headache that won't stop. To treat someone who is suffering from a migraine caused by a palga spirit—or even just any migraine—say the following divine names seven times over a bucket of water and a container of sesame oil:

YoQoWaRehYo YoAh QoWaBehYo PehRehWaYoTaWa
MehNuSaSa AhBehLaAh NuAhTaHe TaTaMehSaYoHeh
QoTaWaMehSaHeh ShiTaWaTaMehHehYoHeh. I charge you,

palga spirit, to leave N, child of N, and to get away from here and do not return. Amen Amen Selah.

Then pour the water over the individual's head, but instead of just dumping it over them, pour it gently over them with something like a ladle. Dry them off gently, and then rub their head with the oil. Do this once a day for three days. Write an amulet for them to wear or carry on them that says:

I charge you, palga spirit, to leave N, child of N, and to get away from here. Amen Amen Selah.

The next two charms concern reptiles. The first treats the physical harm of having been bitten by a venomous reptile. The second deals with harm caused by a supernatural reptile or, as it is called in the manuscript, a "distress charm" sent by another magic worker (an "evil sorcerer"). The divine names that are applied to damage done by the **bite of a venomous reptile** are HehYoWaLaHehWa TsaBehAh-WaTa HehWaZaQoTehAhHeh TehWaSaYoAhHeh RehTaYoBeh, and they should be said over the actual wound or over a container of vinegar that the client then drinks. It's a good idea to mix that vinegar with water at least half and half and to ensure the container is a small one, as drinking straight vinegar can irritate the throat. Or after saying the names over it, use it to dress some vegetables that the person eats. Also, remember to always combine action in the material world with magical action for best results. If a person gets bitten by a venomous reptile, they should be treated by a health-care worker as well as a magic worker.

Another spell that concerns reptiles is not about dealing with the aftermath of a bite by a venomous snake or lizard but rather an attack that features a **magical or supernatural reptile**. Since this spell also focuses on what are called "distress charms," I'm thinking that perhaps the client sees reptiles around, most likely in their home or in a dream, or even feels invisible reptiles biting them and is frightened by this, which is its intent, as such supernatural reptiles and distress charms are created and sent to terrorize people by other magicians ("evil sorcerers" again). In this case, the charm against it is to say over the person: HehYoWaLaHehWa TsaBehAhWaTa HehWaZaQoTeh-AhHeh TehWaSaYoAhHeh RehTaYoBeh. I would think this would have to be repeated until the attack ceases, and it would be good to also do a protection charm of some kind, most especially an amulet.

Most magic workers who take on clients have had the experience of someone coming to them to get hexes or cursework removed. This can be difficult, especially because sometimes it's clear that there is no spellwork that's been done against the person; they simply have an odd fixation about being cursed. Often these folks have made the rounds of all sorts of workers and, according to them, have gotten no relief. To my mind, this is not usually evidence of a strong curse but instead of mental illness. Also, I find it's asking for a problem down the road if you take on a client who insists on detailing the long history of all the workers who have failed to release them from this horrific curse. In the past I have told such folks that I can't help them and to go to someone else, and if they ask for a name, I have a couple times given them the name of someone I don't especially like. Other times, I've referred them to folks who are clearly skilled in dealing with difficult cases.

On the other hand, plenty of people have actually been cursed and in an extremely persistent way—an ex is often the culprit, because so many of them just can't let go. In that case, you can do it yourself, or if you don't want to, you can certainly pass them along to someone who is more experienced in extracting pestiferous spirits.

But you might want to try to help someone even if you feel there is nothing supernatural involved and they are simply **suffering from fear or self-doubt**. In that case, this spell offers the double whammy of spoken and written divine names, which I believe would be reassuring to a client.

First, you say the divine names over a container of water that you then "cast over" the person. You don't have to dump a bucket of water over them like it's some Internet challenge. Instead, you could say the names over a bottle of water with a sprinkle top and asperge the bewitched person with it,* or you could use a mister, which is nice because you can give it to the client to take home with them. You could also put the water in a bottle and let them add it to a purifying bath, which they then pour over themselves from head to foot while standing in a washbasin rather than throwing it into a tub. After air-drying, they can get dressed and take the basin outside so they can throw out the water safely away from their home and their loved ones.

---

* You could even use an herb asperger, a typical one being a bunch of fresh hyssop tied together, which is quite traditional and would fit well with *The Sword*, even though Our Hyssop (the *Hyssopus officinalis* of the witches of Europe and North America) is not the same critter as Biblical hyssop (*Origanum syriacum*). But for so many centuries European magicians have been using Our Hyssop in place of the hyssop in the Hebrew Bible that I think it is totally acceptable to make that substitution. It is as if an egregore has arisen around Our Hyssop. Also, there is a certain drama involved in asperging with a bundle of fresh hyssop that in contrast to a bottle with a sprinkle top adds power to the spell, in my opinion—and probably for a client as well. There is nothing like a good prop. And it smells good!

For the written part of the spell, write out the list of divine names on a piece of paper they can fold up and carry with them in their wallet or pocket. You can write it on leather or engrave it on metal if you want, but paper put into a plastic lanyard dingus works well too. If they normally wear a lanyard for work, all the better; just pop it in the back.

These are the divine words to be spoken over the water: AhPeh-WaNuYo BehReh AhPeh WaPeh WaNuYo AhDaNuYo AhGiTehMeh-Teh BehReh ShiEi*NuQoTehSa ShiBehRehWaSaYoAh BehReh Beh-TaGiGiHehWaSa AhDaAhSa QoZaAhSa BehReh AhGiTaShi.

This is what is to be written as an amulet for the client to carry or wear:

אפוני   בר אפופוני אדני
אנטמט בר שעקטם
שברוסיא בר
בתנהוס בר
אנתש

If you are trying **to figure out why someone is sick** but you're unable to, and therefore you can't come up with a spell that would be good to heal them, boil some beer and mix it with water. Say the following divine names over the mixture: AhSaHehAhLa YoWaYo WaShiRehYoAhLa ZaAhTaHehAhLa YoWaWaYo AhTaYoAhLa WaWaYo AhLaYoAhLa YoWaHehWaHeh AhNuTaYoAaLa YoWa-HehWaYo MehLaTaYoAhLa YoYoWa WaHeh. Give this to the ill

---

* Ei like eye for AYIN

person to drink when they are thirsty. It isn't clear if this is meant to cure them or simply comfort them.

Having addressed some issues with human beings in need of healing, we come to a spell about healing the land. If you have fruit trees or date palm **trees that are not producing fruit**, try this spell, but remember that almost all fruit-producing trees take time off and might well produce fruit for one year and then nothing for one to three years. Your non-yielding trees might just be resting from the work of producing fruit. But if you want to help them along or perhaps nag them a bit—and has there ever been a gardener who did *not* nag their plants?—use this spell. Get a new terra-cotta flowerpot* and break it up. Take a large piece—or more than one, depending on how many trees you have to work with—and write the following on it and then bury it next to the roots of the nonproducing tree(s). I think a fine marker is the perfect tool for this job:

פנכיר בר בסנבים פנביר
בר פסנכיר אגתלמו
בר ניתצגס אהסמו
בר אפדני
דודיאה אשכולם׳
צהומתי כאסיי גילגדאי
שהנוסיא קתילתיו אסדוהי

---

* These are cheap, especially the small ones, but you can use any clay vessel that's convenient.

Protection Spells

The next group of spells to look at are for protection, and that can mean protection of a client or of oneself.

This spell directly addresses **magical attack** that causes physical damage to a person thrown by another magician rather than a spirit or the evil eye. Just so we know, we are told that the attack is coming from an "evil sorcerer," but the exact nature of the injury isn't described. Since the water is poured over the client's head, it would seem that the damage done is some kind of head pain or perhaps psychological malady. I well remember helping a client who was targeted by an "evil sorcerer" hired by their ex and who was suffering horrific nightmares of mass deaths. This was one of those times when the magic was almost palpable as a kind of irritating buzzing around the injured person perceptible to others, even if they were not involved with magic themselves or in any way psychic. Although we ended up making an Archangel Michael talisman, this spell would have been a great help, especially if it were repeated periodically.

Like most Sword spells, it is fairly simple. We say the divine names over seven unglazed containers of river water and then pour them over the client's head. This is another occasion where you would not want to dump a bucket over the client's head but instead use a smaller vessel that allows you to pour the water gently. It would be good to do this outside so that none of the water, with its freight of negativity, remains in the house. The client should wear light, loose clothing, like a nightshirt, or go naked. Don't get the water on you. These are the names to be said over the water: HehWaTaMeh-Wa TsaNuAhWaKhe PehHehSaGi TsaBehAhWaTa QoShiNuTsa SaNuYoSaQoDa PehYoShiNuTaYo SaGiTehSaYoYo.

Sometimes your roof needs fixing and you can't afford to do it right then or you can't get someone to do it at that time. *The Sword* offers a fix—a spell **to have rain stop falling on your roof**. Notice that this is not a normal spell for a general halting of rain, say, to cause a drought or, conversely, to stop flooding. That kind of spell would, in my opinion, take a lot more energy than this very focused and local magic. Also, you don't want to be responsible for a drought (just a titch selfish, I would think), and you might well have a garden or plantings you want to take care of even as you protect your house. This spell limits itself to the area of your roof. You write the spell out on whatever you wish. *The Sword* does not give advice about what to do then, and most probably you simply keep it in your house. But I would advise going a bit further and putting the paper with the writing on it into a plastic bag to keep off water, of course, and to make concrete the spell—repelling water. Then put the baggie in the eaves of your roof, or if you have a tile or shingle roof, tuck it underneath one of them. Don't forget to remove it when it's time to get the roof fixed. Then you can simply say the divine names in reverse order and tear up the paper and throw it out.

אסא נרמע קריפו אברו
בבריך פסייי יה פיגוד עדו
פוכן פוכפיקן וא הוהא

This next spell is a bit frightening because it addresses the issue of **a group of people wanting to attack you**, to the extent that they will be unafraid to come to your house. It seems to be based on the idea of a confusion spell, since it exchanges material from one place with another. I think that's a brilliant solution to this issue. Instead of building your house up into a fortress, have the attackers get mixed up and go to some intersection in town where they have no idea what to do.

You take dust from within your house and go to some "paths" in town. For this purpose, I would suggest busy intersections in town. If you have an idea of where these people might be coming from, a busy intersection in that area would be more focused.

At the intersection, say over your house dust the following seven times and then throw it into the intersection and walk away: YoQoWaTaNuYo BehReh AhKaTaTaHehWaHeh DaHehDa-WaSa AhNuTaTaKhehSa AhDaWaNuYoShiAh YoKhehMehNuYo AhQoTaRehSa. You've thus identified this distant intersection and your house.

Shortly thereafter—I'm thinking on the same day—gather dust from a busy intersection in town—but not the same one you used before—and take it home with you. Say the same divine names over it and throw it into your house.

This sounds like a perfect confusion spell to me.

Lots of magical practices provide ways to make someone go away, and we even know spells where something is sprinkled or left on the doorstep of the target. This spell allows you **to banish some-one** by saying divine names over some oil and then smearing it or even just throwing it on the target's gatepost—or a driveway would work. The divine names to be said over the oil are: ShiAhYoLaSa ShiAhYoLaSaYoWaNu MehSaYoNuYoYoHeh BehReh MehSaReh HehYoHeh YoWaAhWaSa YoHehWaKheShi WaHehWaTa ShiTeh-Qo SaShiNuSaHehYo.

To protect yourself from the evil eye, go out on a clear night when you can see the stars and silently write the following names on a piece of leather. Put this amulet into a container made of palm leaves—which is really more like a basket. I have often seen these as small boxes in craft stores. The spell doesn't describe what to do with the box once you put the amulet in it, but I am thinking that since it is intended to protect you from the evil eye, you should take it home with you and put it in a safe place. These are the words to write on the piece of leather.

עפפיה זדוקזנאל

עצציה דינהאל

עצקהיה מכזהיאל

עתריה בשנתנאל

עקתריה נרלהוהיאל

עצשיה יבטטענאל

In various practices, an iron knife is intended for blood work and cursing. For this bit of **offensive protection**, you get a new iron knife and say the following divine names over it: BehTaQo-ShiNuYoAhLa EiTsaSaYoHeh BehSaPehYoPehAhLa NuYoTaQoNuAhLa EiTsaNu-YoHeh HehSaTaYoAhLa EiTaSaMehYoHeh NuYoQoWaTsaYoAhLa NuEiLaTsaYoHeh. When the knife is charged with the names, throw it in the direction of the people you would like to defend yourself from. This doesn't mean you have to approach them face-to-face. It can mean that if they live southeast of you, you go out in your yard and toss it to the southeast. By the way, this would also work **to cut off a relationship with someone**.

To protect yourself from **someone who grabs hold of you to attack you** and wants to murder you, bend the little finger of your left hand and say the following divine names: KaLaLaYo SaTaNu-YoAhLa EiTsaHehWaHeh NuWaTaYoTaHehYoAhLa EiTsaRehYoHeh NuDaRehWaHehYoAhLa EiTsaGiYoHeh Beh-DaYoZaWaHehYoAhLa EiTsaBehYoHeh SaSaTehRehAhLa EiTsaAh Heh-YoHeh HehDaYoMehYoAhLa AhHehWaHeh. When you do so, your attacker will flee you as if you were his killer. This might work just on the basis of psychology alone—any attacker who sees you crooking your little finger and saying what sounds like non-sense, especially if you pronounce it loudly, with power, will probably think you are deranged. In my experience, acting crazy can really help during a street hassle, which is what this spell seems to describe. Also, try it in a situation that can involve, for instance, **someone trying to kill your reputation**, perhaps at work or in a group.

The following spell is for helping you **to pull yourself out of a fire you've fallen into**, but I think this might be very helpful if you are **suffering from a fever**. Say the following divine names to escape safely from the fire: HehDaSaWaMehMehAhYoAhLa AhNu-TaNuAhYoAhLa LaHehYoAhYoAhLa QoTaWaHehGiAhYoAhLa. Another possible use for this simple spell would be **for dousing the flames of obsession or fury**, whether your own or others'.

This spell is designed **to help you if you fall into a deep pit** that you did not see in front of you. Say the following divine names as you are falling, and you will not come to harm:

SaMehQoTaYoAhYoAhLa Shi-GiTehSaAhYoAhLa EiNuTaYoAh-
YoAhLa SaHehGiYoAhYoAhLa ShiRehQoTaAhYoAhLa HehMeh-
GiGiYoAhYoAhLa. I think this should be tried **for depression** and
perhaps as **a respite from grief**.

Try this spell **when you are overwhelmed** with work or when
the pressures of your life are getting to be like a pack of wild dogs
yapping around you. It is intended to save you **if you are drowning** in a deep river. It also feels like it would help **deflect a love
spell** someone has thrown at you or your client. Say: HehMehGiGi-
YoAhYoAhLa ShiNuYoQoTsaAhYoAhLa ShiLaShiGiYoAhYoAhLa
KaRehShiTehNuYoAhYoAhLa ShiLaAhSaAhYoAhLa.

Give this spell a try if you are crushed by a sudden onslaught
of responsibilities either at work or within your family. It is meant
to help you **escape from a rock- or landslide** that falls on you and
traps you, so I think it would also be helpful **if you are oppressed
by gloom** as well. Say the divine names: MehShiQoWaNuYoAh-
YoAhLa HehWaPehYoHehYoAhYoAhLa QoQoMehAhYoAhLa Ah-
NuSaYoTaAhYoAhLa KheTehNuYoTaYoAhYoAhLa MehNuHeh-
WaSaSaAhYoAhLa.

This is similar to the spell for protecting yourself from someone
who attacks you and wants to kill you, but the divine names used
are different. It's a good spell to try **during legal proceedings** and
any potentially hazardous interactions with the government or its
representatives. It was meant not only to protect you from a king
or judge but also to cause either one of them to turn around and
kill the people who captured you and brought you before them, so
you can see how it might well be effective for a court case. Say the
following and, at the same time, crook the little finger of your left

hand when you are brought before the authorities. There is no reason why you can't say the divine names silently: QoNuYoAhWaSaYoAhYoAhLa ShiPehTsaSaAhYoAhLa YoWaTaMehMehAhYoAhLa NuTaNuTsaAhYoAhLa.

This strong binding spell can also be used metaphorically. It is meant **to freeze in their tracks** a band of marauders that attacks you, so you could try it against muggers, God forbid. As I mentioned above, my experience has been that "acting crazy"—for instance, by reciting a bunch of divine names—does seem to deter would-be jerks on the street.

Most of us will not have to deal with a bunch of highwaymen or bandits or even muggers during our life, but we will probably be faced with a group or clique that comes after us metaphorically, attacking our reputation or launching verbal assaults—whether at work, in our extended family, or in our social life. In that case, turn to the west, the location of death—because this is about stopping them in their tracks—and say the following divine names. They will stop and be bound: BehKaLaHehWaAhYoAhLa HehYoLaKaWaAhYoAhLa QoMehGiYoAhYoAhLa HehNuSaPehWaAh-YoAhLa NuTehMehSaAhYoAhLa SaEiSaSaNuNuYoAhYoAhLa. You can **reverse the binding** when you think it's safe to do so by facing the east, the location of rebirth, and saying the divine names in reverse order: SaEiSaSaNuNuYoAhYoAhLa NuTehMehSaAhYoAhLa HehNuSaPehWaAhYoAhLa QoMehGiYoAhYoAhLa HehYoLaKaWaAhYoAhLa BehKaLaHehWaAhYoAhLa.

Usually in town there are plenty of places **to get a drink of water**, but if you are hiking or just walking out in the wild and can't find water, look up to the sky and recite the following divine names:

QoDaShiYoGiAhYoAhLa KaZaHehWaAhYoAhLa QoSaNuYoAh-YoAhLa YoShiLaAhTehAh-YoAhLa LaHehPehSaAhYoAhLa. A spring or other source of water will be revealed to you.

This spell is dedicated **to providing you with food when you are hungry**. After you look to the heavens and spread your arms to the sky and say the divine words, a heavenly prince will come to you and give you food. I think this must be seen metaphorically, since we already know that angels in this magical system do not eat and especially don't like being around any food outside of plain fresh bread. So I think we have to take the appearance of this heavenly prince to represent a force in one's community or even a higher spiritual power in oneself and to look to that power for help finding food. But first raise your hands to Heaven and say: PehYoZaQoYoHehAhYoAhLa MehYoTaNuHehYoAh-YoAhLa QoSaWaTaGiAhYoAhLa ShiMeh-TaYoAhHehYoAhLa.

This is a binding spell **to catch thieves**. You should put your little finger in your ear and say, "May all thieves and robbers be stuck fast and give up in the name of MehRehGiHehMehWaHeh YoAhLa HehWaYoHeh MehRehGiEiShiSaHehWaAhLa HehWaYo-Heh TehYoTehSaHehWaAhLa HehWa YoHeh AhTehTehHeh-SaHehWaAhLa." The spell doesn't designate which hand to use, but given the other "little finger" spells, I think the left little finger would work to initiate the spell. When you want **to release the thieves** and robbers, don't put your finger in your ear, and say the divine names in reverse order: AhTehTehHehSaHehWaAhLa YoHeh HehWa TehYoTehSaHehWaAhLa HehWaYoHeh MehRehGiEiShiSaHeh-WaAhLa HehWaYoHeh MehRehGiHehMehWaHehYoAhLa.

You might not need the above spell if you use this one **against burglars**. Say the following divine names over a jug of water, and then sprinkle it all around the eaves of your house: AhTeh-TehgWaHehSaHehWaAhLa HehWaYoHeh ZaPehTaRehSaHeh-WaAhLa HehWa YoHeh LaKaYoNuYoPehSaHehYoAhLa HehWa-YoHeh EiGiHehNuHehWaAhLa HehWa YoHeh MehPehSaGiYo-HehWaAhLa HehWaYoHeh. This same spell can also be used to keep invaders from attacking a town. Try adding it to precautions **for keeping out vermin and germs** as well.

Another spell **to prevent incursion into your house** is to sprinkle dust from an anthill around the edges of the house and, while doing so, say the following: MehLaAhKaYoNu QoDaYoShi-YoNu RehBehRehBehYoNu MehKaLa KhaYoLaWaAhTaYoheh Da HehWaHehYo HehWaYoHeh HehYoWaHehHeh WaHehHeh YoHeh AhHeh YoHehHeh: DaQoYoMehYoNu MehNu KaWaReh-SaYoAh DaMehTaQoNu LaHehWaNu QoDaMehWaHehYo LaAhWaDaQoQoAh LaMehShiEiBehDaYo KhehRehBehAh LaMehEiBehDa LaHehWaNu RehShiTaHehWaNu: BehShiMeh MehAhRFehYo KaLa QoRehyYoWhiYoYoA.

This spell **protects you from evil spirits** when you are in a place where they are present, but it can also be used **to exorcise them from someone else.** Say the divine names following and end with "I, [your name], child of [mother or father's name], shall pass through here in peace and not come to any harm." If it's to exorcise another person, just say the divine names over the person. These are: TaWaBehReh TaSaBehReh AhKaNu TehTehHeh MehYoTeh-Sa AhWaLaYo AhGiYoDaWa AhSaQoAh DaYoWaQoTehAhSa LaSaWaSa AhNuTaSa SaDaWaPehYoPehLaAh SaSaAh AhWa AhWa HehWaPehHehAhTehAh HehYoPehWaRehQoSaTehAh MehWaNuNuGiYoDaYoNu: MehNuGiYoNuYo NuTehLaAhSa

DaYoNuYoQoAh DaYoSaWaQoAh GiYoHehYoAh TehAhQoSa
QoWaSaMehWaSa YoHeh HehYoDaRehSaAh.

Knowledge

One thing I really like about Jewish magic is how important spellwork for learning, memory, wisdom, and just general brain/mind
stuff is. I'm not familiar with other paths that raise this to such a level
of concern. In fact, there is an entire body of rituals in Jewish magic,
called the Sar Torah rituals, that are focused on acquiring knowledge
and the ability to remember what you learn. Since so much Jewish
magic involves the use of sacred texts to generate magical words,
and since the Hebrew Bible is often considered to hide the secrets of
making powerful magic, it makes sense that spells for knowledge are
held in high esteem and are often met with. Here are a few.

This spell is **for wisdom**. To attain that, every day for three
months beginning with the month of Nisan, when you say the
Amidah, insert the following after the fourth benediction: "SaEiSa-
TaShiHehAhLa YoHehWaHehHeh SaGiSaWaHehYoAhLa YoHeh-
WaHehHeh ShiShiMehSaRehYoHeh-YoAhLa YoHehWaHehHeh,
may the Holy One open up the gates of wisdom to me so that I can
contemplate what they guard."

This particular spell is interesting for a couple of reasons. One is
that it makes very short work of **calling down a particular heavenly
spirit**. There is nothing here about fasting for three days, purifying
oneself, or praying three times a day, partly because you've already
done that to take control of the divine names that are the motor of
this spell. You just write the divine names indicated on a bay leaf and
then say: "I charge you, Prince Abraxas ('BRKSS),[3] to hurry to me
directly and to tell me all that I need to know. Come willingly and

come now." Then Abraxas will come down from Heaven because he has been bound to you by the Sword. You'll see the prince of heavenly spirits, and he will answer you.

These are the names you should write on the bay leaf to accomplish this. The divine names are relatively few, but still you will have to write small and on both sides of the leaf. Needless to say, choose the biggest bay leaf you can find and write with a fine pen. A fine point marker would work. No color or type of ink is designated, so choose what you'd like that you feel would empower the work. I'm thinking a pen with gold or blue ink would be appropriate for calling down a prince of heavenly spirits.

```
סלני׳   הוה   יהניתיוס   הוה
עפרעוהה  הוה  אסנעוהד  הוה
בתנוסס״   הוה
אסא  נרמע  קריפו
אברו   בבריך פסיי׳י  יה
פ׳עוד  נ׳דו  פוכן  פוכפיקו
וא  הוהא
```

If you want **to adjure one of the heavenly princes** you have charged in the ritual and ask them to teach you everything they know, call upon AhHehYoWaPehSaQoTaYoHeh at 3 a.m. and say: "In the name of the master of all the holy ones, BehShiMeh MehAhRehYo KaLa QoRehYoShiYoYoAh YoAhShiYo KaLa MehLaAhKaYoYoAh BehRehAhHehYo DaEiLaMehAh QoLaTaYoRehAh AhLaYo AhLaYo MehPehYo MehQoRehNuSa KhehTaWaMehYoHeh DaAhRehEiAh Wa-RehWaMehAh BehRehAhYoHehWaNu

DaBehNuYo AhNuShiAh ShiMehShiWaHehYo DaHehWa HehWa-
HehAhHeh WaAh YoHeh WaHeh HehHeh EiYoLaAhHeh AhLaHeh-
Ah DaEiLa Da HehTsa AhNuAh AhTaKhehMehYo BehEiLaMeh-
Ah QoLaWaTaMehYo MehQo-RehAhMeh EiTsaPehHehWaYoYo
ShiShiNuWaHehYoYo: AhTaWaNu YoBehRehNuYoTaTsa EiLaYo
BehKaLa AhTaReh MehRehYo KaWaLaAh BehEiYoNuAh Meh-
NuKaWaNu DaTaEiBehDaWaNu LaYo MehDaEiSa DaAhNuAh
BehShiNuAh DaAhTaWaNu YoKaLaYoTaWaNu LaMehEiBehDa
KaLa YoNuBehWaTaAh YoSaAhMehYoAh WaBehAhRehEiAh
SaAhSa YoHehWa HehYo HehWaHehYo HehWaHeh AhHeh-
Wa WaHehYo YoHeh HehHeh WaHeh HehHehYo YoWaHeh-
Yo HehYo AhHehYo HehYo HehWaHeh YoHehWa HehWaHeh
YoHehWa HehWa YoYoHeh YoHehWa YoHehWa HehHeh Heh-
HehHeh YoHehWa HehWaHehHeh YoHehYo HehWa HehWaHeh
HehWaAhHeh HehWaWaHeh YoHeh HehWa HehWa WaHeh
HehHehWa YoWaHehYoHeh HehHeh YoWaHehYo HehWaHeh
AhHehYoHeh AhHehWa HehWaHeh YoWaHehWa HehYo Heh-
HehWa AhHehYo AhHehHeh HehWaHeh HehWa HehHehYo
HehHeh YoHeh HehHeh WaHeh HehHeh WaYoHeh HehHeh
AhWaHehHeh HehHehYoHehHeh HehHeh HehHeh HehHehWa
YoHehHeh YoHeh HehYo HehHehYo HehHehYo HehHehWaHeh
HehHehYo HehWaHeh AhHehHeh YoHehWa AhLa AhLa YoHeh-
Wa. Send to me (name the desired angel here) so that they show and
teach me everything that they know, and having done so, that they
leave me and return to Heaven."

This spell is for catching even bigger game than a more or less
random heavenly prince. When I first came across this spell, I mis-
read it as being addressed to the "Son of Man," which is a phrase that
occurs in Jewish mysticism and which Christians subsequently took

to mean Jesus. In contrast, in Judaism, "son of man" means human beings in general and especially in terms of our frailty and weakness. When I realized that it said "Prince of Man" instead of "Son of Man," I thought immediately that it must designate Metatron, because that highest of heavenly spirits, who sits directly before the throne, was once a human being—Enoch—the only human whom God ever took bodily up to heaven. This phrase, "Prince of Man," is not mentioned elsewhere in Jewish magic that I have seen, so I believe the Metatron identification is correct. I am not sure, though, why anyone would want to call such an elevated angel. It is as close as you can get to calling down God, which is not ever done in Jewish magic, not least of all because it is exceedingly dangerous. Even the angels are burned by staying too long before the divine throne.

But just in case you *do* want **to summon the Prince of Man**, get your prayer shawl and say the following over it: QoRehSaReh-NuHehYoAhLa YoHehWaHeh MehRehWaSaHehYoAhLa YoHeh-WaHehHeh HehYoWaSaQoHehYoAhLa YoHeh WaHehHeh ShiYo-LaHehYo AhSaHeh-YoAhLa YoHehWaHehHeh. Then that spirit will come down from heaven and you can ask him to reveal to you whatever you want to know.

When you are ready for the Prince of Man to leave, say these divine names: YoHehWaHehHeh AhSaHehYoAhLa ShiYoLaHehYo WaHehHeh YoHeh HehYoWaSaQoHehYoAhLa YoHehWaHeh-Heh MehRehWaSaHehYoAhLa YoHehWahHeh QoRehSaReh-NuHehYoAhLa.

It's especially important when adjuring angels to be in a state of ritual purity, fasting at least on that day after having ritually bathed and wearing clean clothing. Otherwise, you expose yourself to the chance of experiencing heavenly, fiery rage.

Harming or Cursing Spells

As mentioned in the first section of this book, nothing in *The Sword of Moses* cautions us against performing aggressive magic, even to the extent of killing spells. The assumption is that we know what we are doing and the action will be appropriate to the situation. That assumption is embedded, in my opinion, in the whole idea of God's approval for us humans using the angels to perform magic that affects not only the spiritual world but also the physical world, including humans and natural elements. Jewish magic does not have any idea of karma, the Three-Fold Law, the slingshot effect, or other negative reactions for negative magic.

But what if you're a jerk and what you do is not appropriate? You go around putting killing spells on people who cut you off in traffic or clerks who are rude to you at the post office. In other words, you use your magic way out of proportion to the offense. What happens then? Well, God did say "*Mine* are vengeance and payback" (Deut. 32:35).

Personally, I have noticed that magicians who frequently resort to cursework often become obsessed with it and see injury to themselves everywhere. When you are throwing out that much energy for slights, how can you have much left to put toward good things?

Again, it is your decision. You are expected to make righteous choices.

This is a rather elaborate spell **for killing someone**. I suppose that such spells *should* always be elaborate, because killing should never be easy. Also, extended or involved preparation gives you time to thoroughly think over whether killing someone is really necessary. Unlike a lot of other magic, it cannot ever be reversed. Saying the divine names backward will not bring the target back to life. Nor will it erase a mistake. And for me, that is exactly what makes a killing spell problematic, just like capital punishment. You only have to make a mistake once.

Here's my experience.

I remember years ago someone calling me and describing the awful actions of their neighbor, who had destroyed the caller's belongings and hurt and even killed some of their animals. They asked if I would do spellwork to kill that neighbor.

I also had neighbors who had threatened to harm my animals and burn down my house—because witches, ya know, we are so evil, etc.—so it was easy to identify with this caller. I was so incensed by what they said the neighbor had done that I agreed to do the spellwork without even charging them. The caller gave me the neighbor's name and address.

Meanwhile, I explained how the caller could do a binding spell on the pestiferous neighbor using a figure or a photo of the individual, some black wool yarn, and a box with a mirror inside. Burying the box would make for a decent but powerful binding spell that would help protect them from their neighbor.

After I hung up, I got to thinking about it and realized I had no way of knowing if what the caller had told me was true. Maybe the neighbor was innocent. Maybe the neighbor had done these things but only after long ill behavior on the part of the caller. Maybe a lot of stuff that I had no way of knowing.

So I decided to do nothing. I figured if the caller were honest, the binding spell would be enough. The caller never reached out to me again, which was a relief. And I decided that I would never again agree to do a killing curse—not for money and not for charity.

Here's the other part of it. I had known of more than one person I had personally seen do horrific things that might well merit a killing spell. But instead of reacting with such a spell, I used a banishing spell. When they died of natural causes, I felt relieved that I was not tied forever to their death.

It's up to you. Just something to consider.

For this killing spell, you need various items: mud from two banks of a river, seven thorns from a withered fruit tree (wild plums usually have good thorns), a springy branch to make a bow, horsehair to make the bow string, and a cloth bag.

With the mud from two banks of a river, you make a figure. The soil should be clay and stick together. If it doesn't, you can always add some air-dry clay to make it stick. A small figure will work fine.

On this figure you write the name of the enemy. One way to do this is to incise the name into the fresh or dried mud with a needle and let it dry. You can also paint it on dry clay.

Put that figure into the cloth bag.

The original spell calls for seven thorns to be taken from a withered date palm, but that's because date palms were commonly available where *The Sword* was written. An old, diseased plum tree—or if you are in the UK, an old, diseased blackthorn bush—would work well.

Why old and diseased? I believe the idea of magical contamination is in action here. Just as the tree is diseased and dying, the target will become the same.

A strong but springy branch is next, and no specific type of tree or bush is described. A young branch in spring is a good choice. It is not for using repeatedly—you only have to fire it seven times. Yew is a good candidate, since it's widely available as a foundation planting, but make sure you wear gloves when handling it, because the sap is poisonous and will raise welts on your skin. I'm speaking from experience here.

You can actually buy nice horsehair from a horse's tail online. People use it to make hair extensions on their own horses (I think this is so wonderful), so it's widely available and not expensive. You can find it in various lengths, even long enough to make a violin bow (31"). Since no particular length is indicated for the bow you're making, you can choose to make the bow smaller if you need or want to.

To enact the spell, tie the ends of the horsehair to the ends of the springy branch you are using for the bow. Have the figure in the bag with you. Point the bow at the figure in the bag and use the bow to "fire" the seven thorns. Say the following divine names over each thorn before firing it: "AhQoTaRehSa ShiLaWaMehYoMeh MehYo-BehGiSaSa SaHehWaTehTehYoAhYoAh, may N, child of N [if you know the name of their parent; otherwise, use their last name], be injured and die." I suggest crushing the figure in the bag with your foot when you are done and just leaving it there. I would also leave the bow there.

What if someone doesn't deserve to die but does deserve being **afflicted by a sore**? I can think of some. This is the way to give them one. You need a new clay jar or pot with a lid—even a clay teapot would work; just stuff some black wool in the spout. You assemble personal items from seven people and put them in the clay vessel. This could include a shoelace, hair, a pen they use at work, a dirty napkin, a hair tie, a used plastic cup, and so forth.

Why are these seven people involved? I believe it is to borrow their strength for this spell. It does not seem in any way to be intended to harm these seven, so no karma debt occurs, if karma debt even exists.

Once you've got the items in the clay vessel, take it to a place outside of town where horses have never walked—off a path in the woods, for example—and say these divine names: PehRehSaWaSa-Yo HehYoBehLa QoWaSaNu PehNuDaAh DaNuDaAhTa PehYo-DaAhYoSa PehPehNuYoShiYo. Then bury the vessel, but keep some of the soil that was resting atop the container and take it home with you. Either scatter in front of the target or throw it on their threshold.

The following is **another killing spell**, but this one is far less involved than the one with the bow and the thorns and is further-more meant to be embedded in the Amidah, which is a central part of the purification ritual that prepares the magic worker to wield the Sword—and which is also the central prayer of the three-times-daily worship in Judaism. So embedding it this way adds to its magical energy.

I think this is a very good illustration of how this magical path does not impose any ethical standards on the magician. The assump-tion seems to me to be that you, as the magic worker, are knowledge-able enough about the situation that you can decide the justification for such negative actions. For me, the fact that the magic worker is to say this spell right after the section in the Amidah called "Makhni'a Zedim" ("You who overpower the vile ones") particularly indicates this.

Say the following right after the twelfth benediction of the Ami-dah: "May AhSaQoWaHeKhehYoYo strike down N, child of N [if you know their parent's name; if not, just use their last name], in the name of AhPehSaWaMehTa BehReh PehRehGiWaSa SaTaNuWa-TaYo ShiPehTaNuSa TaNuPehSaYoSaYo SaRehPehTehYo."

Just as some spells involving food offerings are meant to evoke love in someone's heart, there are also spells that use food **to magically debilitate a person**. This is one of them. In Judaism, eggs are often associated with death, which is quite the opposite of how they are seen in contemporary culture, where they represent birth and life. A section of the Talmud[4] talks about round things representing death, saying that mourners have no mouth—they tend not to speak, in the estimation of the Sages—and this is why round things like lentils and eggs are appropriate for mourners to eat. Nowadays, I have heard people say that eggs consumed as traditional after-funeral food are meant to comfort because they symbolize the cycle of life and death, but I have not found anything in Jewish writings to back that up. I think this is coming, instead, from ambient popular culture.

I wonder if the death association also has to do with the fact that although eggs come from an animal, they are not meat and they do not normally contain blood. (If they do, they are considered ritually not fit to eat under Jewish law.) They're animal food that is considered neutral in the paradigm of *kashrut*. Blood has huge ritual significance in Judaism—blood = life. Something that originates without blood—as opposed to meat, which is salted in order to remove the blood—might well seem dead or deathly to our ancestors, especially an unfertilized egg, which will never have a blood spot—that is, it will never have life.

Even so, in this spell, you use an egg not to kill someone but rather to make them demented—which we might, unhappily, associate with encroaching death. It seems as though this is meant to be a cooked egg, as you say over the egg BehRehDaQoSa LaHeh-BehNu BehDaRehHehWaSaYo TehTaMehTaYoAh EiYoZaTaYoAh MehLaKaYoQo and hand it to the target to eat.

Several spells in *The Sword* involve broken pieces of clay pots as an instrument. It seems there is nothing about the sherd as a tool that confines it to working either good or evil. In this spell, however, it is definitely not a tool for healing but is instead meant **to destroy someone's house**. You break apart a new and unused clay pot—a small flowerpot is handy—and over one the pieces, say Ah-Kheh-YoTaAh BehAhHehMehYoTaYo KaYoNuYoHehYo MehShiPeh-QoWaHehYo BehYoWaEiYo HehMehTaYoAh LaPehNuYoAhSa AhYoDaWaHehSa ShiLaWaShiGiSaAh AhSaRehWaMehYoSa. Then throw the sherd into the target's house. Throwing it onto their property would, I think, be sufficient. This spell could work not only to cause faults to occur in the structure of the house but also rifts in the relationships between the people who live there.

This next spell is **for getting rid of a judge**. The question is just how "rid" does the judge end up being? Do they simply recuse themselves? Retire? Are they disbarred? Are they hospitalized from an accident? Do they get cancer and die? We don't know. I think the severity depends on what you add to the spell. It might be a bit difficult to carry out, since it involves throwing something at a judge. But I think there are ways around the ruckus that might cause, such as throwing the item in the judge's direction—perhaps even from miles away. The biggest issue would be limiting the effect to one particular judge. You gather dust from an anthill. Since this is not meant as a punishing spell but just a removal of one particular judge from power, it's best to avoid fire ant hills. They didn't have fire ants in the Land of Israel in the first millennium, for one thing, and they would be pretty potent, for another. But if you did happen to want to torment the individual, then dust from a fire ant hill might well be a good choice. Whichever you decide to do, gather fine dirt/dust from the anthill, hopefully without bothering the ants too much. If they are fire ants, sprinkle some cinnamon around the hole; the ants will retreat to their nest. Like most bugs, they don't like strong smells. Then just gather a handful of dirt from around their mound, avoiding the cinnamon—although the cinnamon might actually work to increase the "heat" (strength) of the spell. It's just not mentioned in *The Sword*.

Gather the dust into some kind of container like a small jar to make it easier to work with and to save it until you are ready to throw it. Once you are, say the following over it: YoGiTehWaSa HehWaHeh MehNuEiTsaYo HehWaHeh NuHehRehWaTaTaYoAh HehWaHeh PehRehWaMehMeh HehWaHeh. Go outside and throw the dust in the direction of the judge in question.

With this spell, I think it might also be effective if you use a map. Get a map of the courthouse online, and just print it out. You can even do a satellite view. Write the judge's name on the map in the middle of the courthouse. Go outside with the map and say the divine names over the dust. Then throw it at the judge's name on the map. I would leave it out there for a while. If it's breezy, put a plate over the map when you're done to hold the dust there. When you consider it's been long enough—and I would think twenty-four hours would be plenty long enough—crumple up the map with the dust inside and throw it out—somewhere not inside your house. I think it's never a good idea to have items used for an aggressive spell inside your house. You can bury it, preferably in an area where there's a lot of garbage in order to add power to a spell that knocks someone out of power—you literally make them stink.

Next up is an unusual spell to keep food-associated objects, including ovens, sinks, and pots, from being used—basically, **denying someone the ability to make food in their kitchen**. The fact that this comes with a reversal spell makes me think that it is not necessarily a curse; it could also be a keep-off spell. I think it might be extended to cover other items that you don't want others to use, basically rendering them inoperable until you reverse the spell. Think about someone repeatedly borrowing your power tools and not returning them, for example.

You say the divine words over some earth. This could include clean sand, to make things easier. Bring the earth or sand to where the implements you want to render unusable are, stand in front of them, and say the following divine words: NuPehTehGiNuSa NuTehRehWaSaYo DaWaNuYoQo AhSaYoAh KaTa MehGiYoAh TaTaMehTsaAh ShiSaNuWaTa TehWaGiGiWaTa GiAhMehWaTa SaMehHehWa TaYoTaNu ZaQoNuWaMeh. Then throw the earth toward them—notice, just in the direction and not into or on them. In effect, you are dirtying them magically without actually making them physically dirty. This is so you do not have to ritually clean them later. They will be good to go as soon as you reverse the spell.

If you want **to render them usable again**, spit at them—ritual spitting, by saying "peh peh peh" at them, not actually physically spitting on them—and say the following, which is simply the same names as used to initiate the spell but in reverse order: ZaQoNuWaMeh TaYoTaNu SaMehHehWa GiAhMehWaTa TehWaGiGiWaTa ShiSaNuWaTa TaTaMehTsaAh MehGiYoAh KaTa AhSaYoAh DaWaNuYoQo NuTehRehWaSaYo NuPehTehGiNuSa.

Several spells in *The Sword* concern bringing someone down in society—for instance, the previous spell about causing a judge to lose their prominent position. This spell is **for making people hate someone**. It's interesting that the tool in this case is blood. The spell calls for "let blood," which means blood that flows not from an accident but from bloodletting. In that case, you can use a lancet to pierce your finger and let the blood into some water to give it a little bulk. Say the divine names over it AhSaPehKaLa AhQoTaNuAhYo SaRehWaHehMeh TehBehYoHehSa HehSaDaHehGi ShiHehDaWaDaMeh and pour the mixture on the threshold of the target's home. If you can't get that close or they have a camera at their doorstep, put the bloody water in a balloon and throw it.

With this spell, saying the divine words over some olive oil converts it into a noxious substance that will **cause illness**—although we're not told exactly what kind—to someone who rubs it on themselves. These are the divine names to say: YoTsaYoAhWaSa TaRehWaMehGiTehYo AhKaSaLaSa SaHehNuWaTaYoAh EiLaPehNuTa SaSaQoTaYoNu QoBehLaHehMeh QoTaRehWaTaYo. If you really want to be diabolical about it, you could mix this oil into a gift soap.

We can consider this next spell to be a form of curse magic, since a hard hail can wipe out a field and cause it to be useless for an entire season. Cursing someone's field is a classic of European witchcraft. **To make it hail** in a particular place, get a ring made of iron and lead—or wrap some lead solder around an iron ring—and hang it from something tall, like a tree or a stake or even a fence post, and say the divine names over it: HehYoPehRehWa HehYoPehRehWa AhWaSaRehAaYo SaPehPehYoDaWaNu NuWaPehYoPehYoWaNu MehAhPehPehYoWaNu TaYoWaNu.

This next spell is presented ambiguously, as if it might be for treating land that is not fruitful, but given the process of the spell, I think it is actually about **blighting land**. We get eight jugs or containers—which have to be breakable—from eight houses and fill them with water from eight canals. What if you don't have canals where you live? Then choose creeks or even ditches or gutters during a rainstorm.

To that water we add salt from eight houses and say eight times over those jugs of water the following divine names: AhYoYo AhYo- Yo YoYoYoAh YoYoYoAh HehYo AhYo AhHeh HehHeh YoWaAh- Yo HehYo SaSaGiNuYo PehRehNuGiYo PehRehYoNuGi AaNuYo MehYoKaAhLa YoAhWa GiKaRehYoAhLa AhHeh EiNuYoAhLa YoHeh.

Then take those containers to the land in question and sprinkle two containers over each of the four corners of that plot. Finally, break the containers over eight paths. I think the salt and the breaking indicate the negative aspect of this spell, since salting land was an old practice of conquering armies.

For a spell **to make people who are united fight each other**, gather dust from beneath your left foot and say the following divine names over it: LaWaQoYo YoWaAhLa AhLaTaYoAhLa WaMeh- HehNuTaYoAhLa YoWaYo HehYoAhHeh AhBehNuYoAhLa AhHehMehNuAhLa YoYoWa WaHehYo YoWaQoYoAhLa MehShiQoYoTaAhLa YoHeh. Then throw the dust in their direction, and they will become disunited and take up weapons and battle against each other. You can do this with a map just as well as with the actual physical location.

Sometimes the hate people develop for each other in any organization, not excepting religious ones, can become overwhelming and distort the whole shebang. This spell speaks to that. In order **to terrorize people in your place of worship** (I know—it makes me want to laugh out loud, because I recognize how ridiculous that hate can get), write the following on a lead plate and bury that plate on the west side of the building where the temple or church or lodge is located. I believe this would work just as well for a place of work, etc. And it's a lot less hazardous than going postal.

קבצקיאל אה מסטניאל יח

מסרהיאל הווה שפתיאל

עא והפיסיאל

עה כנטותיאל

עא והתמקיאל

עא

עה

The following spell is another that makes use of a new iron knife but goes farther and involves more control over the brutality of the spell. Say the following divine names over a new iron knife: TaShiHehWaHeYoAhLa EiTsaBehYoHeh BehSaPehYoPehYoAhLa EiTsaYoYoHeh AhRehEiTsaQoRehAhLa EiTsaTehYoHeh HeKaSa-NUYoAhLa EiTsaZaYoHeh ShiWaRehSaYoAhLa EiTsaWaYoHa. Jab the knife point down into the ground until it's almost buried. Put your heel on the butt of the knife and expect that the people you are **targeting will do everything they can to kill each other** until you pull it out of the ground again. This might be especially effective if you do it at a time when you know a meeting is going on with the targets in question.

If you want the fighting to stop, pull the knife out of the ground. If you want them to become peaceable toward each other, after you pull the knife out of the ground, take dust from beneath your right foot and say the divine names in reverse. Throw the dust in their direction, and they will become calm. Say the following: EiTsaWaYoHa ShiWaRehSaYoAhLa EiTsaZaYoHeh HeKaSaNu-YoAhLa EiTsaTeh-YoHeh AhRehEiTsaQoRehAhLa EiTsaYoYoHeh BehSaPehYoPeh-YoAhLa EiTsaBehYoHeh TaShiHehWaHeYoAhLa.

The next spell is the negative of the spell about absorbing everything you hear. The *materia magica* here is a bay leaf. If you want to make someone, probably a competitor of some kind, **forget everything they know**, write their name and the divine names below on a bay leaf and bury it under their doorstep. I would say if you can't do that bury it next to the sidewalk at their front walk.

Love Spells
There are nowhere near as many love spells in *The Sword of Moses* as there are in, for instance, the *Greek Magical Papyri*, but here is one. This spell is a love/sex binding spell, but it assumes that the practitioner is already on good enough terms with the target to have her over. Write the woman's name in your blood on a new lamp. The next time she comes over, say the following divine names to her: AhTaQoNuZa DaWaKhehWaHehNu AhHehYoLaMehWa BehReh

AhDaWaSaAh-YoAh AhHehYoLaMehWaSa BehReh AhHehReh-WaPehYo AhHehDaWaSaYo BehReh AhHehNuWaSaYo. I would think the best way to say this to her would be during foreplay, in the guise of pillow talk. And in that case, this spell is **for cementing the partnership** rather than for forcing a woman to come to you, which is a really creepy sort of spell that is quite prevalent in various magical practices.

The parallel spell **to bind a particular man to oneself** involves getting a new terra-cotta pot and breaking it apart. Take a nice piece and dip it in black myrrh. Say the divine names over it. Leave it somewhere the target will pass or in front of his home and walk away from there without looking back.

But what is "black myrrh"? Some consider that it is just a sort of inferior myrrh that is dark and has less of a scent. It might be dark because it comes from a different species of myrrh that makes darker and less fragrant resin, or it might be dark because it has been too long since it was harvested—it's old and has begun to oxidize. But then, how would you go about dipping anything into chunks of dried resin? Even if you powdered the myrrh, it would not stick to a piece of terra-cotta. And who wants an old, expired myrrh in their love spell? Who wants myrrh at all in a love spell, for that matter, since it is traditionally associated with the dead? In Jewish tradition of the Land of Israel it was used to prepare bodies for burial. (This is why Mary Magdalene is often depicted holding an urn—it's full of myrrh used to prepare Jesus's body.)

Another contender is the fresh resin of *Commiphora gileadensis*, which was a sticky and very fragrant substance smelling like lemon and vanilla with an undertone of myrrh. The problem is that, as far as I know, this tree is basically extinct. I recall reading that the ancient Egyptians grew groves of this tree to ensure its availability for their ritual incense and perfume, but I have never seen it offered for sale anywhere in twenty-two years of making incense, so I doubt that it is still available.

A good substitute is what some people call styrax or liquid benzoin—not storax, which is a whole 'nother critter. This is available as a darkish liquid that smells wonderfully of vanilla and generally balsamic scents. It is thick and sticky and has an intensely good odor, which is always helpful for a love/sex spell, and would easily coat a piece of terra-cotta. It's usually sold dissolved in some alcohol in order for it to flow. So my vote is for liquid benzoin resin.

The divine names to be spoken over the benzoin-dipped sherd are: AhTaYoMehYo BehReh BehAhTaMehYo AhTaYoMehWa BehReh BehAhTaYoHehWaLa AhBehRehGiHehWa RehSaAh BehReh NuHehWaHehYoHehWaSa.

This is a second spell **for getting a woman to**, as the spell says, **"follow" you**. You will need enough of your own blood to be able to write with it. And if you leave it too long, remember the blood will clot and start to smell bad, so it needs to be fresh. I think it would be okay to drop some of your blood into a small amount of water (or alcohol) and to use your fingertip for a pen. Then write your name and her name on her gate and the same on your own gate.

What if you don't have a gate? Write it on the threshold of your own home, even if it's an apartment building, and perhaps the pathway to her door. But don't be a stalker.

That might be a bit challenging with this spell, since once you have written on her gate, you should say in front of it: AhLaYoHehWaSa BehReh ShiHehSaNuYo QoQoTaRehYoAhSa KaLaTaYoTa AhHehYoSaYoAh AhDaWaNuYoHehHeh PehRehYoMehTsaYoYo

AhNuYoHehWaSa   ZaZaHehWaHehSaTehAh   HehHehYoAhSa
GiSaKaYoAh.

Best to be very discreet. No magic in the world will make a
woman go out with a stalker—nor should she.

The following is cast as a spell of **creating affection** instead of
the more typical love spells that involve basically forcing someone—
especially women—to present themselves for sex. If you want to
spark the flame of love in someone's heart, say the following divine
names over a piece of bread: TaMehYoMehSa BehReh HehHeh-
LaEiNu AhShiRehHehTsa NuYoHehNuTsa AhPehNuTeh-YoBeh-
Reh PehEiLaTaZaYo and give it to them to eat. This fits well with
many love spells that are activated by the target eating something the
magic worker prepared. As always, I think adding a bit of honey or
jam to the bread is a good idea that further empowers the spell.

Miscellaneous Spells

Here's a nice, very old-fashioned—as in more than a thousand years
old!—**fishing charm**. Get a terra-cotta pot and break it up. Gather
together the pieces and bring them to your fishing place, along with
some olive leaves,* preferably whole dried leaves which you keep separate until you do the spell. You can buy these from online herb
suppliers. At your fishing spot, place them on the shore, putting the
unglazed sherds down first and then putting the olive leaves over
them. If it's windy, I think it would be fine to kind of mix the sherds
and the leaves together so the wind doesn't blow the leaves away. Then
say the following divine names over the little pile: QoWaQoTaSa
BehReh SaDaWaHehWaSaYo AhBehReh MehMehWaAh BehReh

---

* I believe olive leaves are used because they have a fishlike shape.

YoHehWaTaNuPehAh AhBehReh-MehWa BehReh AhShiNuYo-
HehYo AhKaRehMehYo BehReh AhYoLaMehWa.

If you want **to have a great reputation** in the world, to even be famous, write an amulet made from the following divine names and bury it at your threshold or gate:

דודיאה   אשכולס׳
צהומתי׳ כאס׳׳ גּלגדאי
שהנוס׳א קתילתיו אסדוה׳

If you don't have a flashlight but want some light **to illuminate your work**, write the following on a piece of paper and carry it with you to use as you desire. I think this just begs to be used metaphorically, say, when you are trying to solve a thorny problem or you are dealing with a text that is difficult to understand (shed some light on the subject):

נתהות׳אל
עווא סנעאל
עות
עסתנ׳אל
עפיה
שפצ׳אל
שפיה

The Sword of Moses has plenty of practical spells for humble, ordinary problems. One of them is this spell **for someone going bald** or whose hair just won't grow, for instance, in a beard. In that case, the magician should say the divine words over a bottle of nut oil that the client—or maybe the magician themselves—uses to rub on their scalp, or face for a beard. A good nut oil would be almond oil, since almonds are often grown in the area that produced this book. The divine names to be said over the almond oil are ShiQoBehSa HehWaHeh SaRehGiQoNuAhSa HehWaHe TaPehSaNuRehNuYo HehWaHeh QoDaLaWaTaYoAh HehWaHe QoSaBeh ShiNuYoAh HehWaHeh.

Finally, **for a general spell** not covered above, try the following for all other things that are not referred to explicitly. Say, "In the name of the master of all the holy ones BehShiMeh MehAhRehYo KaLa QoRehYoShiYoYoAh YoAhShiYo KaLa MehLaAhKaYoYoAh BehRehAhHehYo DaEiLaMehAh QoLaTaYoRehAh AhLaYo AhLaYo MehPehYo MehQoRehNuSa KhehTaWa-MehYoHeh DaAhRehEiAh WaRehWaMehAh BehRehAhYoHehWaNu DaBeh-NuYo AhNuShiAh ShiMehShiWaHehYo DaHehWa HehWaHeh AhHeh WaAh YoHeh WaHeh HehHeh EiYoLaAhHeh AhLaHeh-Ah DaEiLa Da HehTsa AhNuAh AhTaKhehMehYo BehEiLaMeh-Ah QoLaWaTaMehYo MehQoRehAhMeh EiTsaPehHehWaYoYo ShiShiNuWaHehYoYo: AhTaWaNu YoBehRehNuYoTaTsa EiLaYo BehKaLa AhTaReh MehRehYo KaWaLaAh BehEiYoNuAh Meh-NuKaWaNu DaTaEiBehDaWaNu LaYo MehDaEiSa DaAhNuAh BehShiNuAh DaAhTaWaNu YoKaLaYoTaWaNu LaMehEiBehDa KaLa YoNuBehWaTaAh YoSaAhMehYoAh WaBehAhRehEiAh SaAhSa YoHehWa HehYo HehWaHehYo HehWaHeh AhHeh-Wa WaHehYo YoHeh HehHeh WaHeh HehHehYo YoWaHeh-

Yo HehYo AhHehYo HehYo HehWaHeh YoHehWa HehWaHeh YoHehWa HehWa YoYoHeh YoHehWa YoHehWa HehHeh Heh- HehHeh YoHehWa HehWaHehHeh YoHehYo HehWa HehWaHeh HehWaAhHeh HehWaWaHeh YoHeh HehWa HehWa WaHeh HehHehWa YoWaHehYoHeh HehHeh YoWaHehYo HehWaHeh AhHehYoHeh AhHehWa HehWaHeh YoWaHehWa HehYo Heh- HehWa AhHehYo AhHehHeh HehWaHeh HehWa HehHehYo HehHeh YoHeh HehHeh WaHeh HehHeh WaYoHeh HehHeh AhWaHehHeh HehHehYoHehHeh HehHeh HehHeh HehHehWa YoHehHeh YoHeh HehYo HehHehYo HehHehYo HehHehWaHeh HehHehYo HehWaHeh AhHehHeh YoHehWa AhLa AhLa YoHeh- Wa." This is a longy, but a goody.

For amulets, always start with "in the name of the master of all the holy ones."

בשם מארי כל קדישׁיא

Path-Jumping

Path-jumping is a type of Jewish magic that involves traveling with supernatural help. It is first described in the Hebrew Bible, where God lifts up an individual and sets them down somewhere else far away, as a kind of favor. In that case, it isn't actually magic at all but a divine act—something not done by the person who travels but by God. But by the time of the Talmud, path-jumping meant that you could use divine names to shorten your trip.

In the descriptions of path-jumping in the Talmud, we aren't told exactly how it's done, just that divine names were used. Later, we get the actual formulas as this concept moves out of religious texts and commentaries and into actual magic works.

To some extent, path-jumping in Jewish magic is about getting from one place to another quickly—and faster than would be humanly possible. But the medieval rabbi Rashi said that it was not about the individual traveling faster but about the earth or the sea actually contracting, because the phrase usually used, *kefitsat ha-derekh*, is translated to mean "shrinking the way."[5]

The first example we have of someone using a divine name to shrink the path is in the Talmud, Sanhedrin 95a–b, when a general uses a divine name to rescue King David from Goliath's brother. There are others, most oddly Lilith, who in the *Alphabet of Ben Sira* used a divine name to flee from Adam.[6] That's pretty interesting when you think about it—it implies that God was on her side, not Adam's. In fact, I've noticed that generally divine names in Jewish magic work for all sorts of things that we might think God would disapprove of.

The Sword is the first description of path-jumping that involves some kind of tool in addition to divine names in order to shrink the path. In this case, it's a reed. In later descriptions, the reed has seven knots, then the divine names are written down and stuffed into the middle knot of the reed and one gets on and flies off. Still later, the magic worker has to do certain actions with the reed at certain times, so it all becomes more complicated as we approach modern times. It's odd how as any practice approaches modern times it becomes more complex instead of less so.

We are told that Rabbi Eleazar of Worms, who is sometimes said to be the actual author of the *The Book of Abramelin the Mage*, was reputed to fly on a cloud, and although he himself didn't claim that he did so in his writing, he does give the formula that is said to accomplish this.[7]

Oddly enough, it is in medieval Jewish magic that path-jumping does a U-turn from being an act of God to the magic worker using the "demonic ether"—a special plane inhabited by demons—to transport themselves from one place to another even though divine names are still used to make it happen.[8] One description of how to do this is attributed to Eleazar of Worms and involves writing the divine names on a snakeskin and then wearing it as if it were the arm tefillin, which is pretty blasphemous in this paradigm and fits in with the demonic ether idea.[9] On the other hand, the snake in Jewish magic is sometimes considered to be a creature that flies, on account of the fact that it has no legs.

It's also in the medieval period that we begin to hear about doubles—a professional magic worker of the eleventh century could not only just path-jump but appear in two places at once.[10] Path-jumping evolves into something very similar to what was attributed to European witches: not just flying on some common object, but using a double to travel far while their physical body stays at home, safe and apparently sleeping in bed.[11]

The spell for **path-jumping** in *The Sword* involves a reed, over which you say the divine names AhPehTehYoGiWaNuYoAh TaLa-WaMehTa HehWaHehNuGiEiWaSaYo AhPehHehYoGiQoWaYo ShiYoTaMehWaHehHeh MehHehHehSaWaHeh LaKaWaTa-NuYoAhTa BehReh AhSaNuWaTaTaYoAh RehBeh ShiTsaDaYo RehBeh QoMehWaSa RehBeh AhMehRehSa AhYoNuYoTaHeh-Heh SaGiNuYoHehHeh MehLaTaYoHehHeh. Because of later descriptions of riding a reed in Jewish magic, I would advise getting astride the reed.

Here's another **path-jumping** spell that relates to water and extends the use of the divine names to an object. It packs a double whammy of engraving the divine names pertinent to this spell on a lead plate to be carried with you and tucked into your belt like a weapon. At the same time, as you walk into the water, you say the divine names aloud. For this spell, they are: HehBehQo-ShiPehHehYoAhLa YoHehWaHehHeh EiSaRehGiHehYoAhLa YoHehWaHehHeh HehTsaEiSaNuHehYoAhLa YoHehWaHehHeh MehWaDaDaGiHehYoAhLa YoHehWaHehHeh. This is what you should write on the lead plate:

חבקשפהיאל יהוה
עסרנהיאל יהוה
הצעסנהיאל יהוה
מודדנהיאל יהוה

If you are going somewhere and get lost, say the following divine words over the four corners of your garment or your prayer shawl to make the way clear. Of course, this means you have to have a four-cornered garment on you. You can do this with a scarf you are wearing—not one you just carry in your pocket—or you can wear a tallit katan when you are planning to go somewhere you are not familiar with or when you are setting off somewhere and are just unsure of the way. Since some other spells involve the use of a four-cornered garment, it might be helpful to have one. These are the words to say: SaAhDaMehWaGi BehReh BehYoSaTaNuYoAh DaWaSaYo HehSaYo DaMehSaTehGi SaGiNuSaYoYo AhPehYoSa-TaNuYo DaWaTaAhHeh TehYoSaWaSa QoWaSaTehRehSaWaSa AhPehLaGiYo MehPehLaGiYoMeh AhYo AhWaTaWaTaBehReh AhWahTaWaTa QoDaWaSaYoAh AhQoWaTaGi.

The next path-jumping spell also involves the use of a four-cornered garment. The spell is meant to enable the magic worker **to travel over the sea as if it were dry land**. Does that mean it gives you the ability to walk on water? Or is the intention to prevent you from drowning if your boat gets wrecked? I am not sure, nor is it clear whether you should say this before you even board the boat, if you are expected to say it as a wreck is happening, or if we are intended to think we will walk on the water. Most of the time, these path-jumping spells simply make the trip feel quicker, but sometimes they are on the level of teleportation. You take one of the corners of the four-cornered garment and hold it in your hand. One of the other corners will point ahead of you, and you should say the following divine names: GiSaMehSa BehReh GiYoSaMehWaTeh MehShiTehRehWa MehTaYoYo LaHehSaWaHehKa PehRehNuSa-WaSa AhGiSaSa QoQoTaTa MehHehRehYoGiYo.

The four-cornered garment might be a ritual garment, but it might also be a plain scarf, since in various places in the history of Jewish magic, we are told about someone doing path-jumping by not only using divine names and perhaps riding on a reed, but also covering their head and face with a scarf,[12] much as we might cover our head when praying the Amidah, interestingly enough. A curious connection is that at least one European text describes witches blindfolding themselves to fly to the Sabbat.[13]

Divination

I really like this spell, because it makes use of a garden plant for prediction. It involves a lettuce that grows in a rosette. Any loose leaf lettuce can be used in this way, as well as butterhead lettuce and many other of the heirloom variety lettuces. It is over this type of lettuce head still growing in the ground that you ask **for help in determining whether a journey you are about to take will be successful or not**. This could apply to business or relationships. Go out on a sunny day and say the divine words as you stand in front of the plant: GiSaKaYoAh PehRehTaNuYoAh MehBehAhTaSaYo AhPehWaPehYoAh AhNuPehNuYo BehSaTehYo. You should stay and watch the leaves of the lettuce. If they remain nice and firm, then you should go ahead and take the trip because you will succeed, but if the leaves wither or get limp, you shouldn't go because the trip will not profit you.

The next spell reminds me of this use of the lettuce to find out if your journey will be a success or not. In this case, though, the position of the individual's head is the determiner of a good outcome or a bad one. **If a person is ill and you would like to know whether they will recover or succumb to their illness**, say over them the divine names NuAhSaTehGi RehWaPehNuYoHehWaSa ShiYoReh-MehTehYo AhShiMehGiYo ShiLaTaTaHehNu SaHehTehNuYo YoShiQoWaSa PehNuHehWaSa TehWaKaYoMeh YoYoHehWaSa-YoYo. If they turn to you, they will recover. If they turn away, they will die. Oddly enough, I have often read in old stories that people who are dying will turn to the wall. And I have noticed this in animals as well. It is as if looking at and paying attention to other living beings in the room is too much for them at that point and they have to concentrate on the work of dying, may the gods bless them.

Freeing Prisoners

It's surprising how many ancient spells are about getting someone out of prison. I'm not sure if imprisonment occurred more often in ancient times or if nowadays we are just ashamed to say we know someone in prison and care enough about them to do a magical working to get them out. Certainly in the United States, we have a far greater percentage of people in prison than any other nation in the world,[14] so we might expect there is a strong call for spells to get people out of prison.

This spell is three-pronged, and you have to be able to visit the prisoner. But unlike some of the other spells in *The Sword* that deal with **freeing prisoners**, this does not involve any material at all. Instead, you say the divine names three times: once in front of the prisoner, once outside in front of the prison, and once standing before the sun. Say these words: AhSaDaWaSa AhTehRehYoTaYoTa AhShi-TehTaYoAh DaMehGiSaSaYoAh WaSaPehDaNuWaSa GiHeh-WaShiTeh.

It can't hurt, and it lets the prisoner know you are doing what you can to help.

The other way to use this spell is to free someone from a metaphorical prison, such as intrusive thoughts or neurotic fears that prevent them from living a full life—or at least a life they would like to live.

Another way **to get someone out of prison** is to make a candy of gum arabic and dates and say over it the divine names: SaDaHeh-WaMehYo YoHehWaHehYo AhTaGiMehYo HehWaHehYo SaHeh ShiMehTaNuYo HehWaHeh TehRehWaMehTsaHehYoYo HehWa-HehHeh TaTaLaYoWaHehYo. Have the prisoner eat these in order for them to be released.

CONCLUSION

The Sword of Solomon might be an old book, but it has plenty to offer us magic workers all these centuries later. Especially interesting is just how independent the magic worker can be, even when working within a religious tradition. For instance, if a magician has sufficient knowledge of the Hebrew Bible, they can discover their own words of power in it instead of just relying on the ones listed in this work. The implication is, after all, that the magician who wrote this book not only borrowed divine names from amulets and so forth but also created their own, thanks to attaining deep knowledge of the Hebrew Bible through magical means—or even simply through deep study. I think this can be applied to other sacred texts as well.

The Sword displays just how organized a professional magician needs to be in order to have access to all the possibilities they are capable of exploiting. This is not a system where the magic worker picks something out of the air; instead, it has strong organizational aspects that value making information readily available to the magical practitioner through the use of something as mundane as an index, which this work clearly had at one point. That points to practices like keeping a commonplace book, which involves creating a table of contents as it is being written in, as opposed to a Book of Shadows that has to be paged through to find things. The organization necessary to be a good magician is also manifested in just how much discipline is required for the magic worker to complete the purification ritual before working with the divine names.

Although nowadays plenty of magical practices warn of dire consequences for doing negative magic or cursework, as I've said before, we don't find that in *The Sword*. *We* have to take responsibility for our actions and we don't live in God's playpen; that ended when we left the Garden. The version of God supported by *The Sword* doesn't protect us from our own stupidity, vanity, or arrogance. We have to learn that on our own.

Furthermore, not only does God not forbid magic, but in this magical system, God expressly gives us permission to do it. And that magic is not limited to "white" magic but also includes "black" magic. This is even though working with demons is not involved. To me, that makes *The Sword* a quintessentially gray practice.

I particularly like that the purification ritual that protects us from angelic wrath makes of them more partners than servants. They are bound to work with us as long as we don't smell bad—which is our half of the bargain. It is not our magical skill that enables us, or when we were born, or whether we were born with a caul, but strictly the divine words and our purification.

There are no secrets here, no whispers of family tradition or lodge secret sauce. It is not about our place in time or in society. It is just us and the words. I think in that way the Sword of *The Sword* is most palpable; we take it on through purification and we alone must heft it. We learn it and it is ours, both the white and black of it.

It is also appealing that this book describes a magical practice that has a lot of similarities to witchcraft: it calls for almost no sophisticated or costly props and instead relies on common materials because the real power is in the words, not the stuff. This is the magic of middle-class people who can read and write, but not that of the functionaries of princes or of high society. There are no elaborate rituals with masks and fancy robes. Furthermore, it doesn't require the practitioner to live in a big city where all sorts of materials or props would be for sale. You can reside in a hut at the edge of town if you want. For me, *The Sword* has a strongly shamanistic or witchy flavor as opposed to sorcery. Even many of the spells sound like Early Modern European witchcraft—stopping ships, blighting fields, healing, and cursing.

The other side of that is that it does not say anything about the magician's spiritual level. I've noticed that much so-called high magic today demands that the magic worker develop their spirituality or soul or whatever we'd like to call it and in some way to elevate or refine it. There is none of that here. Even though we can do this magic because of God's names and we are required to pray as part of the three-day purification, that purification is not a heightening of our spirit. It doesn't set us above our fellow humans or make our souls refined. It's basically just a spiritual bath so we can talk to the angels. We are still ordinary people; only we are magicians instead of merchants or tradespeople. For me, this lack of elitism is refreshing.

It is interesting that there are no spells for attaining wealth, finding treasure, or success in gambling. This implies that the magic worker doesn't have a money problem and doesn't attract people who do. That in turn implies a slightly better-off clientele than laborers.

I like that it provided people with a work-around to the power of the rabbis in the past—a way to have a decent position in society and to make a living without having to be part of the rabbinical system, which could be quite problematic because of rivalries and hereditary crap. As a magic worker using *The Sword*, you could be respected in your community no matter whom you had descended from and no matter if you had never learned anything in a house of study. You could provide a good and necessary service and make a living, all without being a part of the system—even with rejecting that system altogether.

The Sword doesn't demand that we work with demons in any way—although these angels can be just as dangerous.

There is almost no animal sacrifice, unlike in the *Greek Magical Papyri* or other magic paths then and even now. The divine names have more power than killing any animal does, no matter how fancy the ritual knife. The words are a sword that is fundamentally kick-ass, having been involved in the creation of the universe.

The primary motor of the magic in *The Sword* is not the magician or their material tools but the words. The words are even more important in the magic than the angels are.

My life has been blessed by working with this material—surprisingly, in a spiritual way, with the realization that to a great extent, the names here and the angels *are* the Divine. I found that a Divine that has an endlessly scintillating body is so much easier to connect with for me than one that is described with human characteristics. Maybe for me it's also the idea that the words are central and the motor of the magic that fits me and my life.

I have been very gratified, for instance, in finding that my hunch that the words in the Sword held graphical possibilities that would add power to their magic turned out to be true. This validated my belief in the power of art, of the graphical. This connects for me with my life as an artist. It was as if the Sword said to me that yes, there is great power to be found in form and beauty; they are valid and powerful pursuits.

I think there is a great deal in *The Sword* that is useful to the present-day magical practitioner. I hope *The Sword* touches you in the way it has me—with a sense of a profound power at one's fingertips that is not so far away up in heaven, but rather here and now, in spoken and written words, in humble materials, that can heal or kill.

NOTES

INTRODUCTION

1. M. Gaster, PhD, *The Sword of Moses: An Ancient Book of Magic, From an Unique Manuscript, with Introduction, Translation, an Index of Mystical Names, and a Facsimile* (London: D. Nutt, 1896).

BACKGROUND OF *THE SWORD OF MOSES*

1. Yuval Harari, "Moses, the Sword, and *The Sword of Moses:* Between Rabbinical and Magical Traditions," *Jewish Studies Quarterly* 12, no. 4 (2005): 294.

2. Yuval Harari, "The Sword of Moses (Ḥarba de-Moshe): A New Translation and Introduction," *Magic, Ritual, and Witchcraft* 7, no. 1 (May 2012): 58.

3. Yuval Harari, *Jewish Magic before the Rise of Kabbalah*, translated by Batya Stein (Detroit: Wayne State UP, 2017): 256.

4. Harari, *Jewish Magic*, 257.

5. Harari, *Jewish Magic*, 259.

6. Harari, *Jewish Magic*, 378.

7. Harari, *Jewish Magic*, 242.

8. Harari, *Jewish Magic*, 234.

9. Harari, *Jewish Magic*, 249.

10. Harari, *Jewish Magic*, 246.

11. Harari, *Jewish Magic*, 248.

12. Harari, *Jewish Magic*, 250.

13. Shaul Shaked, "Dramatis Personae in the Jewish Magic Texts: Some Differences between Incantation Bowls and Geniza Magic," *Jewish Studies Quarterly* 13, no. 4 (2006): 363.

14. Shaked, "Dramatis Personae," 364.

15. Shaked, "Dramatis Personae," 364.

16. Harari, *Jewish Magic*, 281.

17. Harari, *Jewish Magic*, 281.

18. Harari, *Jewish Magic*, 284.

19. Harari, *Jewish Magic*, 276.

20. Harari, *Jewish Magic*, 280.

21. Harari, *Jewish Magic*, 260.

22. Harari, *Jewish Magic*, 70.

23. Harari, *Jewish Magic*, 172.

24. Harari, *Jewish Magic*, 326.

25. Harari, *Jewish Magic*, 326.

26. Harari, "Sword," 67.

27. Gideon Bohak, *Ancient Jewish Magic: A History* (Cambridge, UK: Cambridge University Press, 2011): 341.

28. Hagigah 15b.

29. Moshe Idel, *Ascensions on High in Jewish Mysticism: Pillars, Lines, Ladders* (Budapest and New York: Central European University Press, 2005): 31.

30. Harari, "Moses," 301.

31. Harari, "Moses," 301.

32. Harari, "Moses," 301.

33. Ithamar Gruenwald, *Apocalyptic and Merkavah Mysticism* (Leiden, Netherlands: Brill, 1980): 176.

34. Harari, "Moses," 303, where Yuval Harari states that Rachel Elior gave him the idea that Horeb might be a corruption of *harba*.

35. Harari, "Moses," 303.

36. Harari, "Moses," 324.

37. Harari, "Moses," 304.

38. Harari, "Moses," 304.

39. Harari, "Moses," 305.

40. Harari, "Moses," 306.

41. Harari, "Moses," 312.

42. Harari, *Jewish Magic*, 180.

43. Harari, *Jewish Magic*, 194, n. 5.

44. Shaked, "Dramatis Personae," 371.

45. Harari, *Jewish Magic*, 197.

46. Harari, *Jewish Magic*, 198.

47. Harari, *Jewish Magic*, 195.

48. Harari, *Jewish Magic*, 190.

49. Harari, "Sword," 58.

50. Harari, "Sword," 67.

51. A collection of homilies about various sections of the Hebrew Bible, composed around 845 CE.

52. Michael D. Swartz, "'Like the Ministering Angels': Ritual and Purity in Early Jewish Mysticism and Magic," *AJS Review* 19, no. 2 (1994): 158.

53. Swartz, "'Like the Ministering Angels,'" 159.

54. Shabbat 88b–89a.

55. Harari, "Sword," 60.

56. Harari, "Moses," 321.

57. Harari, "Moses," 327.

58. Yuval Harari, "Havdala de-Rabbi Akiba," in *The Encyclopedia of Ancient History*, first edition, edited by Roger S. Bagnall, Kai Brodersen, Craige B. Champion, Andrew Erskine, and Sabine R. Huebner (Chichester, UK: Blackwell Publishing 2013), print pages 3084–85.

59. Harari, *Jewish Magic*, 173.

WHO WROTE IT, WHEN, AND WHERE

1. Bohak, *Ancient Jewish Magic*, 176.

2. Shaked, "Dramatis Personae," 365.

3. Harari, "Sword," 61.

4. Harari, "Sword," 65.

5. Harari, "Sword," 66.

6. Harari, "Sword," 66.

7. Bohak, *Ancient Jewish Magic*, 175.

8. Harari, *Jewish Magic*, 284.

9. Moses Gaster, "The Sword of Moses." In *Studies and Texts in Folklore, Magic, Medieval Romance, Hebrew Apocrypha, and Samaritan Archaeology*, vol. 1: 288–337, vol. 3: 69–103 (KTAV: Brooklyn, 1971).

10. Harari, "Sword," 63.

11. Harari, "Moses," 296.

12. Harari, "Sword," 63.

13. Harari, "Sword," 69.

14. Bohak, *Ancient Jewish Magic*, 224–25.

15. Harari, *Jewish Magic*, 338.

16. Idel, *Ascensions*, 34.

17. Idel, *Ascensions*, 35.

18. Harari, "Sword," 66.

19. Bohak, *Ancient Jewish Magic*, 341.

20. Harari, "Sword," 69.

21. Harari, "Sword," 66.

22. Harari, "Sword," 65. If the author had known Greek, it would not have been necessary to write the same spell again in Jewish Babylonian Aramaic.

23. Bohak, *Ancient Jewish Magic*, 178.

24. Bohak, *Ancient Jewish Magic*, 178.

25. Bohak, *Ancient Jewish Magic*, 178.

26. William M. Brashear, "The Greek Magical Papyri: An Introduction and Survey; Annotated Bibliography (1928-1994)," *Band 18/5. Teilband Religion. Heidentum: Die religiösen Verhältnisse in den Provinzen (Forts.)*, edited by Wolfgang Haase (Berlin, Boston: De Gruyter, 2016): 3577.

27. Harari, "Moses," 300 n. 28.

28. Bohak, *Ancient Jewish Magic*, 252.

29. Bohak, *Ancient Jewish Magic*, 263.

30. Bohak, *Ancient Jewish Magic*, 286.

31. Bohak, *Ancient Jewish Magic*, 289.

32. Harari, "Sword," 69.

33. Harari, "Sword," 69.

34. Harari, "Sword," 69.

35. Harari, *Jewish Magic*, 274.

36. See Moshe Idel, *Golem: Jewish Magical and Mystical Traditions on the Artificial Anthropoid*, SUNY Series in Judaica: Hermeneutics, Mysticism, and Religion (Albany: State University of New York Press, 1990).

THE STRUCTURE OF
THE SWORD OF MOSES

1. Bohak, *Ancient Jewish Magic*, 177.

2. Eyal Regev, "Pure Individualism: The Idea of Non-Priestly Purity in Ancient Judaism," *Journal for the Study of Judaism in*

the Persian, Hellenistic, and Roman Period 31, no. 2 (2000): 176.

3. Regev, "Pure Individualism," 176.

4. Regev, "Pure Individualism," 176.

5. Regev, "Pure Individualism," 184.

6. Regev, "Pure Individualism," 181.

7. Regev, "Pure Individualism," 179.

8. Regev, "Pure Individualism," 187.

9. Regev, "Pure Individualism," 192.

10. Regev, "Pure Individualism," 192.

11. Regev, "Pure Individualism," 195.

12. Regev, "Pure Individualism," 197.

13. Swartz, "'Like the Ministering Angels,'" 140.

14. Swartz, "'Like the Ministering Angels,'" 142.

15. Swartz, "'Like the Ministering Angels,'" 137.

16. Swartz, "'Like the Ministering Angels,'" 145.

17. Swartz, "'Like the Ministering Angels,'" 147.

18. Swartz, "'Like the Ministering Angels,'" 147.

19. Swartz, "'Like the Ministering Angels,'" 147.

20. Swartz, "'Like the Ministering Angels,'" 148.

21. Swartz, "'Like the Ministering Angels,'" 148.

22. Swartz, "'Like the Ministering Angels,'" 149.

23. Swartz, "'Like the Ministering Angels,'" 149.

24. Swartz, "'Like the Ministering Angels,'" 149.

25. Swartz, "'Like the Ministering Angels,'" 152.

26. Swartz, "'Like the Ministering Angels,'" 151.

27. Swartz, "'Like the Ministering Angels,'" 151.

28. Swartz, "'Like the Ministering Angels,'" 154.

29. Swartz, "'Like the Ministering Angels,'" 154.

30. Swartz, "'Like the Ministering Angels,'" 137.

31. Swartz, "'Like the Ministering Angels,'" 138.

32. Swartz, "'Like the Ministering Angels,'" 139.

33. Swartz, "'Like the Ministering Angels,'" 155.

34. Swartz, "'Like the Ministering Angels,'" 165.

35. Swartz, "'Like the Ministering Angels,'" 157.

36. Swartz, "'Like the Ministering Angels,'" 157.

37. An ascension text written between 650 and 1050 CE.

38. Swartz, "'Like the Ministering Angels,'" 160.

39. Rebecca Lesses, *Ritual Practices to Gain Power: Angels, Incantations, and Revelation in Early Jewish Mysticism* (Harrisburg, PA: Trinity Press International, 1998): 118.

40. Lesses, *Ritual Practices*, 119.

41. Lesses, *Ritual Practices*, 120–22.

42. Lesses, *Ritual Practices*, 130.

43. Lesses, *Ritual Practices*, 132.

44. Lesses, *Ritual Practices*, 134–35.

45. Lesses, *Ritual Practices*, 135.

46. Lesses, *Ritual Practices*, 137.

47. Lesses, *Ritual Practices*, 147.

48. Lesses, *Ritual Practices*, 155.

49. Lesses, *Ritual Practices*, 157.

50. Lesses, *Ritual Practices*, 156.

51. Lesses, *Ritual Practices*, 156.

52. Lesses, *Ritual Practices*, 160.

53. Swartz, "'Like the Ministering Angels,'" 137.

54. Harari, "Sword," 61.

55. David Frankfurter, "Narrating Power: The Theory and Practice of the Magical *Historiola* in Ritual Spells," Chapter 22 in *Ancient Magic and Ritual Power*, edited by Paul Mirecki (Leiden, Netherlands: Brill, 1995): 457.

56. Frankfurter, "Narrating Power," 459.

57. Frankfurter, "Narrating Power," 459.

58. Frankfurter, "Narrating Power," 460.

59. Frankfurter, "Narrating Power," 460.

60. Frankfurter, "Narrating Power," 462.

61. Frankfurter, "Narrating Power," 470.

62. Frankfurter, "Narrating Power," 470.

63. Frankfurter, "Narrating Power," 463.

64. Frankfurter, "Narrating Power," 469.

65. Frankfurter, "Narrating Power," 471–72.

66. Frankfurter, "Narrating Power," 471–72.

67. Frankfurter, "Narrating Power," 474.

68. Harari, *Jewish Magic*, 288.

69. Harari, "Sword," 59.

70. Harari, "Moses," 295.

71. Harari, *Jewish Magic*, 288.

72. Harari, "Sword," 61.

73. Joseph Yahalom, "Angels Do Not Understand Aramaic: On the Literary Use of Jewish Palestinian Aramaic in Late Antiquity," *Journal of Jewish Studies* 47:1 (Spring 1996): 34.

74. Michael D. Swartz, "Jewish Magic in Late Antiquity," in *The Cambridge History of Judaism*, pp. 699–720, edited by S. Katz (Cambridge, UK: Cambridge University Press, 2006): 708.

75. Bohak, *Ancient Jewish Magic*, 176.

76. Bohak, *Ancient Jewish Magic*, 176.

77. Michael D. Swartz, *Mystical Prayer in Ancient Judaism: An Analysis of Ma'aseh Merkavah* (London: Coronet Books, 1991): 238.

78. *Sefer ha-Malbush, The Book of the Garment*, translated by J. P. Feliciano; *academia.edu*.

79. Bar-Ilan, Meir, "Magic Seals on the Body among Jews in the First Centuries C.E.," *Tarbitz* (Mandel Institute for Jewish Studies) 1 (1987): 37–50. In Hebrew only, but the abstract is in English.

80. Bohak, *Ancient Jewish Magic*, 177.

81. Bohak, *Ancient Jewish Magic*, 177.

82. Harari, "Moses," 294.

83. Harari, *Jewish Magic*, 213.

84. Harari, "Sword," 69.

85. Harari, "Sword," 62.

86. "Oral tradition," in *A Dictionary of the Bible*, edited by W. R. F. Browning. Oxford Biblical Studies Online, accessed February 17, 2021; *oxfordbiblicalstudies.com*.

87. Michael D. Swartz, "Scribal Magic and Its Rhetoric: Formal Patterns in Medieval Hebrew and Aramaic Incantation Texts from the Cairo Genizah." *The Harvard Theological Review* 83, no. 2 (1990): 165.

88. Swartz, "Scribal Magic," 166.

89. Swartz, "Scribal Magic," 171.

90. Swartz, "Scribal Magic," 171.

91. Swartz, "Scribal Magic," 171.

92. Swartz, "Scribal Magic," 172. Swartz believes that this same formula ended up in Greek magical texts.

93. Swartz, "Scribal Magic," 172.

94. Swartz, "Scribal Magic," 179.

95. Swartz, "Scribal Magic," 179.

96. Swartz, "Scribal Magic," 179.

97. Swartz, "Scribal Magic," 179.

98. Harari, *Jewish Magic*, 226.

99. Harari, *Jewish Magic*, 216.

100. Harari, *Jewish Magic*, 217.

101. Bohak, *Ancient Jewish Magic*, 177.

102. Bohak, *Ancient Jewish Magic*, 319.

103. Harari, "Sword," 64.

104. Harari, *Jewish Magic*, 352.

105. Harari, *Jewish Magic*, 353.

106. Harari, *Jewish Magic*, 340.

107. Harari, *Jewish Magic*, 355.

108. Harari, *Jewish Magic*, 357.

109. Harari, *Jewish Magic*, 370.

WORKING TO WIELD THE SWORD

1. *opensiddur.org/about-this-project/policies/copyright-policy/*.

2. Weekday Private Amidah, by Rabbi Shoshana Meira Friedman (e Creative Commons Attribution-ShareAlike (CC BY-SA) 4.0 International copyleft license), modified by Harold Roth; *opensiddur.org*.

3. Psalms 91:1–2.

THE SPELLS

1. Harari, *Jewish Magic*, 190.

2. Joseph Naveh and Shaul Shaked, *Amulets and Magic Bowls: Aramaic Incantations of Late Antiquity* (Skokie, IL: Varda Books, 2009): 127 n.3.

3. For abraxas/abrasax, see W. M. Brashear, "The Greek Magical Papyri: An Introduction and Survey; Annotated Bibliography (1928–1994)," *ANRW* II.18.5 (1995): 3380–3684 (at 3577).

4. Bava Batra 16b.

5. Mark Verman and Shulamit H. Adler, "Path Jumping in the Jewish Magical Tradition," *Jewish Studies Quarterly* 1, no. 2 (1993): 133.

6. Verman and Adler, "Path Jumping," 135.

7. Verman and Adler, "Path Jumping," 136.

8. Verman and Adler, "Path Jumping," 137.

9. Verman and Adler, "Path Jumping," 139.

10. Verman and Adler, "Path Jumping," 138.

11. See Claude Lecouteux, *Witches, Werewolves, and Fairies: Shapeshifters and Astral Doubles in the Middle Ages* (Rochester, VT: Inner Traditions, 2003).

12. Verman and Adler, "Path Jumping," 141.

13. Carlo Ginzburg, *Ecstasies: Deciphering the Witches' Sabbath* (Chicago: University of Chicago Press 1991): 132.

14. Comparison of US Incarceration Rate with Other Countries; *en.wikipedia.org.*

REFERENCES

Bohak, Gideon. *Ancient Jewish Magic: A History.* Cambridge, UK: Cambridge University Press, 2011.

Brashear, William M. "The Greek Magical Papyri: An Introduction and Survey; Annotated Bibliography (1928–1994)." *Band 18/5. Teilband Religion. Heidentum: Die religiösen Verhältnisse in den Provinzen (Forts.),* edited by Wolfgang Haase. Berlin, Boston: De Gruyter, 2016.

Frankfurter, David. "Narrating Power: The Theory and Practice of the Magical *Historiola* in Ritual Spells." Chapter 22 in *Ancient Magic and Ritual Power,* edited by Paul Mirecki. Leiden, Netherlands: Brill, 1995.

Ginzburg, Carlo. *Ecstasies: Deciphering the Witches' Sabbath.* Chicago: University of Chicago Press 1991.

Gruenwald, Ithamar. *Apocalyptic and Merkavah Mysticism.* Leiden, Netherlands: Brill, 1980.

Harari, Yuval. "Havdala de-Rabbi Akiba." In *The Encyclopedia of Ancient History,* first edition, edited by Roger S. Bagnall, Kai Brodersen, Craige B. Champion, Andrew Erskine, and Sabine R. Huebner. Chichester, UK: Blackwell Publishing 2013.

Harari, Yuval. *Jewish Magic Before the Rise of Kabbalah.* Translated by Batya Stein. Detroit: Wayne State University Press, 2017.

Harari, Yuval. "Moses, the Sword, and *The Sword of Moses:* Between Rabbinical and Magical Traditions." *Jewish Studies Quarterly* 12, no. 4 (2005): 293–329.

Harari, Yuval. "The Sword of Moses (Ḥarba de-Moshe): A New Translation and Introduction." *Magic, Ritual, and Witchcraft* 7, no. 1 (May 2012): 58–98.

Idel, Moshe. *Ascensions on High in Jewish Mysticism: Pillars, Lines, Ladders.* Budapest and New York: Central European University Press, 2005.

Idel, Moshe. *Golem: Jewish Magical and Mystical Traditions on the Artificial Anthropoid.* SUNY Series in Judaica: Hermeneutics, Mysticism, and Religion. Albany: State University of New York Press, 1990.

Lecouteux, Claude. *Witches, Werewolves, and Fairies: Shapeshifters and Astral Doubles in the Middle Ages.* Rochester, VT: Inner Traditions, 2003.

Lesses, Rebecca. *Ritual Practices to Gain Power: Angels, Incantations, and Revelation in Early Jewish Mysticism.* Harrisburg, PA: Trinity Press International, 1998.

Meir, Bar-Ilan. "Magic Seals on the Body among Jews in the First Centuries C.E." *Tarbitz* (Mandel Institute for Jewish Studies) 1 (1987): 37–50. In Hebrew only, but the abstract is in English.

Regev, Eyal. "Pure Individualism: The Idea of Non-Priestly Purity in Ancient Judaism." *Journal for the Study of Judaism in the Persian, Hellenistic, and Roman Period* 31, no. 2 (2000): 176–202.

Shaked, Shaul. "Dramatis Personae in the Jewish Magic Texts: Some Differences between Incantation Bowls and Geniza Magic." *Jewish Studies Quarterly* 13, no. 4 (2006): 363–87.

Swartz, Michael D. "Jewish Magic in Late Antiquity." In *The Cambridge History of Judaism*, pp. 699–720, edited by S. Katz. Cambridge, UK: Cambridge University Press, 2006.

Swartz, Michael D. "'Like the Ministering Angels': Ritual and Purity in Early Jewish Mysticism and Magic." *AJS Review* 19, no. 2 (1994): 135–67.

Swartz, Michael D. "Scribal Magic and Its Rhetoric: Formal Patterns in Medieval Hebrew and Aramaic Incantation Texts from the Cairo Genizah." *The Harvard Theological Review* 83, no. 2 (1990): 163–80.

Verman, Mark, and Shulamit H. Adler. "Path Jumping in the Jewish Magical Tradition." *Jewish Studies Quarterly* 1, no. 2 (1993): 131–48.

Yahalom, Joseph. "Angels Do Not Understand Aramaic: On the Literary Use of Jewish Palestinian Aramaic in Late Antiquity." *Journal of Jewish Studies* 47:1 (Spring 1996): 33–44.

INDEX OF SPELLS

ABOUT THE AUTHOR

Harold Roth

Harold Roth is an author and artist, and among the foremost authorities on plants within the modern occult community. He has studied Hebrew as well as Jewish magic and mysticism for decades. The author of *The Witching Herbs,* Harold teaches classes on botanical magic, Kabbalah, and witchcraft. Visit him at *haroldroth.com* and follow him on Instagram and Twitter @haroldrothart.

TO OUR READERS

Weiser Books, an imprint of Red Wheel/Weiser, publishes books across the entire spectrum of occult, esoteric, speculative, and New Age subjects. Our mission is to publish quality books that will make a difference in people's lives without advocating any one particular path or field of study. We value the integrity, originality, and depth of knowledge of our authors.

Our readers are our most important resource, and we appreciate your input, suggestions, and ideas about what you would like to see published.

Visit our website at *www.redwheelweiser.com*, where you can learn about our upcoming books and free downloads, and also find links to sign up for our newsletter and exclusive offers.

You can also contact us at *info@rwwbooks.com* or at

Red Wheel/Weiser, LLC
65 Parker Street, Suite 7
Newburyport, MA 01950